SUB-SAHARAN AFRICA

INTERNATIONAL RELATIONS INFORMATION GUIDE SERIES

Series Editor: Garold W. Thumm, Professor of Government and Chairman of the Department, Bates College, Lewiston, Maine

Also in the International Relations Series:

ARMS CONTROL AND MILITARY POLICY—*Edited by Donald F. Bletz**

EASTERN EUROPE—*Edited by Robin Remington**

ECONOMICS AND FOREIGN POLICY—*Edited by Mark A. Amstutz**

THE EUROPEAN COMMUNITY—*Edited by J. Bryan Collester**

INTELLIGENCE, ESPIONAGE, COUNTERESPIONAGE, AND COVERT OPERATIONS—*Edited by Paul W. Blackstock and Frank Schaf, Jr.**

INTERNATIONAL AND REGIONAL POLITICS IN THE MIDDLE EAST AND NORTH AFRICA—*Edited by Ann Schulz*

INTERNATIONAL ORGANIZATIONS—*Edited by Alexine Atherton*

LATIN AMERICA—*Edited by John J. Finan**

THE MULTINATIONAL CORPORATION—*Edited by Helga Hernes*

POLITICAL DEVELOPMENT—*Edited by Arpad von Lazar and Bruce Magid**

SOUTH ASIA—*Edited by Richard J. Kozicki**

SOUTHEAST ASIA—*Edited by Richard Butwell**

THE STUDY OF INTERNATIONAL RELATIONS—*Edited by Robert L. Pfaltzgraff, Jr.*

U.S.S.R.—*Edited by David Williams and Karen Williams**

U.S. INVOLVEMENT IN VIETNAM—*Edited by Allan W. Cameron*

*In preparation

The above series is part of the
GALE INFORMATION GUIDE LIBRARY

The Library consists of a number of separate series of guides covering major areas in the social sciences, humanities, and current affairs.

General Editor: Paul Wasserman, Professor and former Dean, School of Library and Information Services, University of Maryland

Managing Editor: Dedria Bryfonski, Gale Research Company

SUB-SAHARAN AFRICA

A GUIDE TO INFORMATION SOURCES

Volume 3 in the International Relations Information Guide Series

W.A.E. Skurnik

Professor of Political Science
University of Colorado, Boulder

Gale Research Company
Book Tower, Detroit, Michigan 48226

Library of Congress Cataloging in Publication Data

Skurnik, W   A   E
   Sub-Saharan Africa

   (International relations information guide series ;
no. 3)   (Gale information guide library)
   1. Africa, Sub-Saharan--Bibliography. 2. Africa,
Sub-Saharan--Foreign relations--Bibliography.— I. Title.
Z3501.S55 [DT351]   016.32767   73-17513
ISBN 0-8103-1391-X

For Peggy, Ian, and Colin

VITA

W.A.E. Skurnik is a professor of political science at the University of Colorado, Boulder. He received his B.A., M.A., and Ph.D. in political science from the University of Pennsylvania.

Skurnik traveled in West Africa for research as a Penfield Scholar for International Relations, attended conferences on African studies in the United States and Africa, was a Fulbright-Hays lecturer in West Africa in the spring of 1976, and is a member of the African and Middle Eastern Studies Program at the Universities of Colorado and Denver. He has written many articles and book reviews for various journals on African affairs. Some of his publications on Africa include THE FOREIGN POLICY OF SENEGAL; AFRICAN POLITICAL THOUGHT: LUMUMBA, MKRUMAH, AND TOURE (editor); and SOLDIER AND STATE IN AFRICA (coauthor).

CONTENTS

Introduction ix

Chapter 1 - Pan-Africanism, Unity, and Foreign Policy 1
    A. Substantive Introduction 1
    B. General International Relations 11
    C. Unity and Pan-Africanism 18
    D. Foreign Policy and Diplomacy 24

Chapter 2 - Western Europe and Africa 31
    A. Substantive Introduction 31
    B. Economic Relations 41
    C. France 43
    D. Great Britain 45
    E. Portugal 46

Chapter 3 - The United States and Africa 49
    A. Substantive Introduction 49
    B. General Literature 59
    C. Congressional Documents 64

Chapter 4 - The Socialist Countries and Africa 69
    A. Substantive Introduction 69
    B. The Soviet Union and Eastern Europe 79
    C. The People's Republic of China 81

Chapter 5 - African Liberation Movements 83
    A. Substantive Introduction 83
    B. Liberation Movements 93

Chapter 6 - Reference Works 99
    A. General Bibliographies 99
    B. Bibliographic Essays 103
    C. Handbooks 105
    D. Who's Who 108
    E. United States Government Documents 109
        i. Department of State 109
        ii. Department of Commerce 112

Contents

    F. Serials 113
    G. Library List 116

Author Index 117

Title Index 121

Subject Index 127

INTRODUCTION

Most of the countries of sub-Saharan Africa have been independent in their present form for fifteen years or less. Scholars and observers tend to view the international relations behavior of these new states as novel and assume that the behavior of these states differs from that of older, more established states. Some recent observers suggest that such differences in behavior result from special circumstances rather than from fundamental departures. The study of the international relations and foreign policy behavior of sub-Saharan Africa is nevertheless sufficiently fresh, challenging, and promising, from the points of view of both substance and methodology, that it will attract increasing attention.

This volume consists of two parts. The first focuses on the major problems and questions examined in the literature and revealed by state behavior. Chapters in this part begin with essays which cover substantive developments as they are known from the public record and comment on various perspectives and methodological concerns as they are expressed in available commentary. The essays also provide a broad perspective sometimes lacking in specialized monographs and are designed for nonspecialists in the field, such as government officials, business executives, and students. Moreover, persons such as anthropologists or specialists in literature, who do not concentrate on international relations, may find the essays useful in providing a structure for understanding human phenomena different from that of their discipline. Unless otherwise specified, quotations in the text are followed by the author's last name and an abbreviated title; the full citations are listed alphabetically in the bibliographic sections which follow the substantive introductions. Each chapter is followed by an annotated bibliography, which is further divided into subject matter according to the available literature.

The second part of this book lists bibliographies of various reference works, with annotations and comments to direct users to information on specific topics. Entries in both parts were chosen largely for their availability in American public or university libraries; therefore, few references to works in languages other than English are included.

The chapter on American policy (section C) lists forty-five congressional documents issued between 1957 and 1974 relating to policy toward Africa. These documents contain a wealth of information on a variety of topics and provide fruitful data for research. To my knowledge, no other such listing is readily available.

The essays in this Guide do not always faithfully reproduce the priorities of other writers on Africa. The requirements of perspective, combined with the need to compress material into a page or paragraph, do not accommodate more than highlights. But the essays were nevertheless written also to encourage further thought and to place one's convictions, or awareness of Africa, against a larger canvas. The brevity and fluidity of Africa's impact on and participation in the world system only add to the rewards of further study.

Chapter 1
PAN-AFRICANISM, UNITY, AND FOREIGN POLICY

A. SUBSTANTIVE INTRODUCTION

Pan-Africanism has been seen by both African and foreign commentators as an overarching concept whose foundations include wishful thinking, utopianism, and ideological commitment. The idea is slowly being grounded in realities. Pan-Africanism can be a perplexing subject. The term is protean, and can mean an idea, a feeling, an ideal, or a structure. The classic introduction to the subject in English defines it as "a movement of ideas and emotions" (Legum, PAN-AFRICANISM) and then turns to a kaleidoscope of events outside of and inside Africa to review its growth.

The book surveys the roots of pan-Africanism (emotions of the black world, exile, ambivalence toward the West, inferiority complexes, pride in color, longing for a forgotten past); the growth of the diaspora (conferences and declarations, and transplantation to Britain); and its return to Africa between 1958 and 1962 (more conferences, nonstate structures, rival groups of African states, and eventual rejection of continental political unification). One African intellectual described pan-Africanists as "trying to be profound about the obvious" (Jansen, NONALIGNMENT, p. 275).

The literature on pan-Africanism usually focuses on its sources, contents, objectives, and structural manifestations. Pan-Africanism has been seen as resulting from a spiritual affinity among Africans, a common heritage of African traditions, and a long history of oppression at the hands of non-Africans, which created alienation among Africans and a search for identity. Much of pan-Africanism is thus a conscious rejection of the colonial situation, exploitation, and the denial of human dignity. The theme of unity which underlies much of pan-Africanism has its roots in two phenomena: one is the immense social, economic, and political diversity of traditional and colonial Africa, and the other is the dispersal of some of its people. Because it is based partly on a notion of race, it can be termed race-conscious, although it is not racist.

The contents of pan-Africanism can be considered a series of myths and assumptions, taken as self-evident and hence not requiring logical demonstration.

1

It can be interpreted specifically as implying a common destiny for all Africans or even all black people, or generally as an unspecified state of mind, but it remains elusive all the same.

One frequent assumption involves an underlying harmony of Africans that will somehow effortlessly rise to the surface to govern inter-African relations. This is perhaps an idealization of an African past presumably free from the shackles of present-day realities. Yet little evidence suggests that the various peoples who identify as Africans did so before foreign contacts. As one prominent African put it, "it took colonialism to inform Africans that they were Africans" (Mazrui, PAX AFRICANA, p. 46). The colonial experience, however, does not distinguish Africans from others who were colonized, and may be a poor basis for examining pan-Africanism.

The objectives of pan-Africanism are as much ideal as real. They are instrumental in the quest for a framework transcending political micronationalism: the search for a philosophy different from others, a mystique of brotherhood and unity, a protest against the arrogance of western tutelage. It is an ideal to which can be attributed no wrong, an invisible mantle which nothing can sully. The extent to which it is used as an object of deference indicates its need as a focus of pride and a psychological firmament providing an additional measure of security. It may not be always reflected in African state behavior, but is nonetheless widely treasured and forms part of the context of African international relations.

Efforts to create inter-African political state structures are frequently interpreted as part of a wider movement toward pan-Africanism. Pan-Africanism remains a powerful ideal. But it is useful to distinguish pan-Africanism as an ideal, on one hand, from elements of African unity as part of reality, on the other. Even then Africa is far from achieving the less remote and more practical objective of political unity. As one observer noted: "African unity remains a slogan . . . yet to be matched by major achievement. Political unification remains the exception rather than the rule" (Welch, DREAM, pp. 356-57).

African leaders have followed two major avenues toward unity. One is political, rooted in constitutional terms but frequently used by one party to manipulate another, or as a tool for political domination. The other avenue is nonpolitical and has involved technical and functional cooperation without the surrender of national sovereignty. The rhetoric which accompanied the creation of a number of short-lived political structures demonstrates the powerful appeal of the ideal. However, African domestic political systems are fragile and fragmented and political leaders discourage pan-African sentiments within their countries, and thus chances for political unification are not bright at this time. It is ironic that pre-independence unity schemes fail because of insufficient state support, and post-independence efforts fail because they are seen as threats to the new states. Many conferences of nongovernmental organizations in the late 1950s met under the banner of pan-Africanism, but such groups eventually gave way to the new states as the major actors in international relations. In reality, there was greater unity in Africa before independence than after it. Political unity remains an attractive objective, but the gap between theory and reality remains wide.

Schemes for interstate unification in Africa can be roughly divided into two time periods: before and after political independence. Before independence, colonial powers created political and quasi-political structures on which genuine African interstate units could have been based. In some cases these reflected primarily the interests of the colonial power or of white settler groups, and it is not surprising that they did not survive. Others, however, redistributed the relative wealth of component territories, as well as relieved the metropole of the burdens of administration and modernization in the colonies. As independence approached, the wealthier territories refused to continue to support their less fortunate neighbors, and these federal structures lapsed. These structures did not accurately reflect the emerging national interests of the new states, or they did so only for the weaker states; hence, they were dissolved or survived only as organs of functional cooperation beset by constant political stress. They fell victim to conflicts between African states and colonial powers, settler interests, and other African states.

National independence has been the greatest barrier to interstate political unification in Africa. This independence has produced three major obstacles to pan-African unification: (1) the priority given to nation-building; (2) strong ideological commitments which make difficult a consensus on rules for conducting international relations; and (3) the emerging personalities of territories, rooted in distinct cultural, social, and political experiences.

The experience of the Mali Federation in 1959 and 1960 was a good example of the effects of competing unification-independence forces. The Mali Federation was a direct outgrowth of the larger federation of French West Africa, established at the turn of the last century by the French government. Paris decided to transfer responsibility for its continuation to the African territories in 1957, when demands for autonomy were growing. When withdrawal of the French was proposed, profound disunities among the Africans were revealed. The Mali Federation was an attempt to save the larger ensemble, but it fell victim to the inter-African disputes. One of its component units, Senegal, took up the fight, chiefly for economic and domestic reasons. The French federation had given that territory a privileged economic position, and Senegal's leaders feared the domestic economic, social, and political repercussions of a sudden loss of income. Senegalese leaders used a mystique of African unity to attract African support and invented the myth of the European "balkanization" of Africa to pressure the French to maintain their support.

The Mali Federation was created officially in June 1959, became independent a year later, and broke apart in August 1960. Two major factors accounted for its short life. One was the basic incompatibility between Senegalese and Soudanese leaders. Because of important differences in their societies, the two leadership groups held widely divergent views on ideology, economic development, suitable political structures, and political style, all of which led to disagreements about the nature and structure of the new Federation. The

3

second major factor was the Soudan's bold attempts to monopolize power, which jarred the Senegalese into dissolving the federal partnership. Soudanese behavior was widely interpreted as an attempt to subvert Senegal from within. They sought control over the armed forces and the federal structure, but also maneuvered inside Senegal to weaken the incumbent government's power base and later tried to involve France and the United Nations. These events were watched by African leaders elsewhere with the greatest interest. The effect was sobering, and these events reinforced the conviction that African unity was desirable and theoretically possible, but that the sovereignty and independence of the territories was more crucial in practice.

Another major development which influenced African views on political unity was the struggle between two mutually antagonistic alliances created at independence, the Casablanca and Brazzaville groups. The former, an association of five states, gathered to mobilize support for ideologically defined positions on the Algerian-French conflict, Moroccan claims for Mauritanian territory, and the proper government in the former Belgian Congo. These issues were eventually settled largely as a result of forces external to Africa, but bitterness and divisiveness remained. The Casablanca challenge was met by the Brazzaville alliance, a much larger group whose chief concern was the establishment of international rules of behavior to provide predictability and security in a fast-changing continent. It was their view that, without prejudice to substantive issues, the honoring of principles of inviolable sovereignty and territorial integrity was a more useful way to achieve harmony and cooperation than was the pursuit of ideological commitment.

One example of a persistent inter-African organization, however, is a defensive organization known as OCAMM (Organisation Commune Africaine, Malgache, et Mauricienne), an outgrowth of the Brazzaville alliance. Agreement on the need to protect the new states is the base of the group. The cement which holds OCAMM together has many ingredients, but the group stresses moderation and realism in international relations and the principle of nonintervention. OCAMM has occasionally become political, not as a matter of policy or intent, but in instances when radical African states held positions which appeared uncompromising and attempted to use the Organization of African Unity (OAU) to bring the majority of moderates into line. For example, when Moise Tshombe became Congolese premier, radical states sought unilaterally and through the OAU to replace him with a more acceptable leader. The majority took the position that, although they might not like Tschombe or what he stood for (and many did not), an independent state had the right to choose its own government and this was too important a principle to be sacrificed to the ancillary question of a particular incumbent. OCAMM viewed such external interference as a dangerous precedent that could increase overall African instability.

Present-day political sensitivities do not hinder all forms of interstate cooperation in Africa. The earlier optimism of pan-Africanist idealism has given way to more practical questions of functional and technical cooperation, taking place in the shade of the political conflicts that tend to dominate the headlines. Numerous nonpolitical regional and continental organizations further cooperation among states, from air travel to economic planning to disease control. OCAMM has encouraged such endeavors, and its members generally increased their mutual trade relations. In east Africa, a number of international technical services have survived political crises. Once the issue of the decolonization of the continent is satisfactorily resolved and once a consensus on interstate behavior is stabilized, these cooperative ventures may multiply. The relatively low interest in Africa by external powers may also make such ventures more likely.

The creation of the Organization of African Unity (OAU) in 1963 was a turning point in African international relations, if only because its membership takes in almost the entire continent, making it one of the world's great regional organizations. In the context of a discussion of political unification, however, the OAU is neither a government nor a supra-national organization. It is mostly a protective device, and its establishment reflected pressing insecurities. Mutual external concerns included Africa's weakness in facing two superpowers fighting an alien, remote cold war, and Africa's relative powerlessness in the international system. At the inter-African level, they concerned the continued dissent which might rigidify and further weaken the continent and the threat of chimerical ventures in political unification which might lead to African versions of imperialism. Finally, there were strong fears of losing novel state independence. The OAU adopted four major guidelines to govern inter-African state relations: the equality of states--protection against other states' supremacy; noninterference in internal affairs--protection from subversion; territorial integrity--protection from arbitrary changes in political frontiers; and peaceful settlement of disputes without an all-African version of a supreme court--protection from encroachments on national sovereignty.

The OAU founding states agreed also on a set of broad foreign relations objectives, including cooperation in accordance with the ideals of the United Nations, extirpation of colonialism from the continent, and a "policy" of nonalignment toward the outside world. Reference to the UN reflected the prestige and usefulness which this body conferred upon its newest members. The UN was, in fact, an irreplaceable forum for getting to know each other and the world; membership was an important badge of sovereignty and full-fledged membership in the international community, as well as a locus for harmonizing views and a channel of influence on issues of common concern.

The stand on colonialism referred to states which had not yet become independent and/or achieved majority rule, primarily the Portuguese territories, Rhodesia, and South Africa. The OAU founding members committed themselves to an ambitious program which included rupture of diplomatic relations with and a "total economic boycott" against Portugal and South Africa, an all-African liberation army, and the unification of African liberation movements in these areas. Although "neocolonialism" is not mentioned in the OAU charter, it was nevertheless on the founders' mind. Africans had reason to be concerned about economic dependence which survived political independence. "Neo-colonialism" has varied meanings. It serves as a roof concept intended to help keep out or expel undesirable foreign influences, actual and perceived. Its specific content varies from economic or other forms of exploitation to the presumed machinations of foreign intelligence services. It can be defined only within a specific context because it rests on the intangible and subjective notion of the desirable. But it symbolizes a continuing search for greater independence and implies the goal of an unspecified degree of actual independence compatible with external dependence.

Reference to nonalignment derived from the attractions of the Indian concept of neutralism and on the need for distance from the effects of big power rivalries on African independence. The term nonalignment is confusing; it has been termed immoral, hypocritical, ignorant, arrogant, or mere ideological fantasy. It is not a policy, for this would require renunciation of external support in foreign relations; it is not neutrality, since involvement in politics means taking sides; it is not necessarily anti-Western, since opposition to colonialism and neocolonialism is grounded in the recent experience of Africa; and it is not necessarily pro-Communist, since, for instance, Russian support and assistance may be a Russian rather than an African decision. Nonalignment is a foreign policy guideline stipulating that African support for, or solicitation of support from, outside powers must not be taken for granted and must result from an independent choice by African sovereign states. To the extent that it stresses that Africans want to make their own decisions, it is an outgrowth of the colonial period. Nonalignment means the absence of automatic support, with the accent on "automatic." For African states it is normal international relations behavior and it seeks to avoid permanent entanglements in a world dominated by larger and more powerful political units.

Nonalignment is no guarantee for sound judgment on all matters of foreign policy. The African states have a right to follow what foreign relations guidelines they prefer but they also need to be free from excessive expectations rooted in misreadings of such vague policy guidelines as nonalignment. Adherence to the principle of nonalignment need not prevent selective alignment on particular issues if it is based on the decision of sovereign African states. In their actual behavior, nonaligned states frequently cluster around specific issues, so that the international state system or important segments thereof may view the nonaligned as just another power bloc.

Although it is too early to judge the eventual function and effectiveness of the OAU, it is nonetheless clear that the organization suffers from several handicaps. Some of these may be attributed to its structure, which resembles the concert of nations model in that collective decisions are not binding and are easily evaded. But there are also major substantive and procedural problems related directly to the nature and dynamics of the societies encased in national boundaries. African states share a basic political, social, ethnic, and economic fragility, and they fear any collective action which may reinforce domestic centrifugal or secessionist tendencies. Such concerns explain the states' reluctance to vest the OAU with significant powers of intervention. The few attempts to help resolve inter-African disputes, some successful, resulted as much from the personal qualities of the African leaders who participated in the mediation process as from an OAU mandate. However, a permanent OAU structure with clear legitimacy has not emerged. A major issue which the OAU has been unable to solve is the tension between the desire for inviolable sovereignty, on one hand, and the costs of a hands-off attitude in cases of civil wars, on the other. In general, the OAU has remained aloof from such issues. This stance results not so much from inability as from the unforeseen and unintended momentum of prior policy decisions presumably laid to rest. But the condoning, unintentionally, of large-scale massacres on the grounds that to do otherwise would violate state sovereignty has produced an egregious blemish on the OAU's international prestige and a severe blow to the image of its effectiveness among Africans.

The OAU's authority is sharply circumscribed by the continued sovereignty of its component states. Its creation also reflected a structural characteristic of inter-African state relations, that of profound divisions on the question of African unity. One group insisted that state sovereignty must be transferred to the OAU, and another, the larger, preferred to leave it with the states. This division has not yet been resolved. It has been suggested that the OAU was unable to increase its slender authority and legitimacy (Thompson, "Legitimacy"). Its legitimacy is constantly called into question, and still rests largely on nothing stronger than the continued desirability of its existence. Its authority was flaunted or disregarded on numerous occasions. What progress it made must be weighed against signs such as plummeting attendance records, reluctance to address potentially divisive issues, and hasty and emotional decisions subsequently disavowed in the capitals of member states. Moreover, external challenges did not galvanize the OAU into sustained or significant action, and at times they weakened the organization. Successive crises in the Middle East, for instance, forced the OAU into positions of questionable benefit for the member states and created a serious rift in the organization. While significant disagreement about the proper functions of the OAU exists, the growth of its legitimacy and authority will be difficult. One close observer comments that, while "united on 'common enemy' issues, the members [are] less inclined to work for positive and concrete links among themselves" (Woronoff, ORGANIZING, p. 637). The disenchantment with the OAU, however, does not foreshadow its demise. Quite the contrary, it likely will remain an important symbol of unity, as well as of pride and dignity, in African international relations.

African international relations in the economic realm have been beset with difficulties. As they undertake modernization, African states are still largely extensions of pre-independence foreign economic ties; their dependence remains substantial, basic, and long-range. Africa became a part of the world economy as a result of initiatives of the colonial powers, and the area's economic activities followed lines deemed most suitable by those powers--agricultural and mineral production for export. The new, modern economic sectors in the territories were not generalized, and instead they remained small enclaves in large subsistence sectors.

Since independence African governments have attempted to tackle simultaneously two major tasks: growth of modern domestic economies and expansion of foreign economic ties. The obstacles to both are immense. Internally, states lack skills needed for rapid modernization. Also, demands for social services, which are not immediately economically productive, are rising faster than ability to meet them. Finally, resentment at continued external dependence is growing. Externally, export markets are expanding slowly and capital and know-how imports are below demand. Grants are viewed as economically unsound or unbecoming the dignity of independence, while loans become heavy burdens exceeding the states' abilities to repay. Investments are needed, but they are keenly resented as unjustly exploitative, and economic decisions are sometimes made on the basis of criteria external to Africa. Moreover, colonial powers conceived economic plans for areas larger than the present separate states, based on links which Africans were unwilling or unable to maintain; political separation makes rational economic planning more difficult.

For a combination of political, psychological, and economic reasons, inter-African development schemes thus far have met with little success. The pooling of economic resources and the creation of a continental authority to implement economic decisions is highly desirable. But the behavior of African states suggests that to work, such cooperation would have to produce immediate, visible, concrete benefits for all at either the continental or small-scale regional level. The economic nationalism which accompanied independence is now dominant in Africa, and inter-African trade generally has either declined or continued as only a small fraction of total external trade. African states have an interest in maintaining and improving many of their economic ties with Western Europe while at the same time seeking to diversify.

Systems theory as an analytical focus in international relations has been applied to Africa, particularly at the regional or subsystem level. Such analysis has several uses, including (1) identifying recurrent patterns of behavior and their structural components; (2) correcting widespread single-factor or otherwise limited analyses; (3) explaining why Africa does not fit neatly into larger discussions of the Third World or global power blocs; and (4) illuminating the relative power relations within given subregions of Africa. A variant of a bipolar model is helpful in explaining the alliances arising in Africa after independence and behavior which tends to persist in less attenuated form even after the formal dissolution of most of these blocs. The tool, as applied to Africa, is a promising framework which deserves further attention. However, as one prominent student of interaction patterns in southern Africa points out, "an eclective approach [remains] imperative for the study of international relations" in Africa (Grundy, CONFRONTATION, p. 303).

The study of foreign policy in Africa has barely begun. Some scholars working in the area suggest that current models for the study of foreign policy behavior are inappropriate and too cumbersome to be applied to the developing states. The foreign policy-making process in the vast majority of African states seems fairly simple. The weakness or absence of domestic societal structures, the

8

nature and occupation of the population, the comparative weakness of military establishments, the paucity of natural resources, and the novelty of diplomatic establishments guide students to consider the two major factors shaping foreign relations to be individual foreign policy decision makers and the external material dependence of these states. This outlook may result from the observer's own value preferences, but is also influenced by the nature of the societies to be investigated. It requires an approach combining ideology (motives of leaders) and attention to material (mostly external) constraints and opportunities. Thus, a guiding principle like opposition to colonialism can be understood as the preference of given leadership groups but also as a policy instrument inherent in the era of decolonization which can be used to propitiate certain types of behavior by external forces.

Students often assess the foreign policy of African states on the basis of their own judgments about African leaders' preferences. This probably relates in part to their desire to influence the foreign relations of the states to which they turn their attention. An example is the controversy over the foreign policy of the Ivory Coast. That country has remained closely aligned with France since its independence in 1960. Critics contend that this involves unacceptable subservience to the former metropole and tends to rob Ivoiriens of their dignity. Others suggest that that country is merely taking full advantage of circumstances and that the Ivory Coast, as it has done in the past, will diversify its foreign relations and decrease its heavy dependence on France at an advantageous time.

Vernon McKay suggests that several broad conflict patterns strongly influence the foreign policy orientation of the new African states. He distinguishes three patterns of conflict to which foreign relations are responsive. The first is domestic. It includes competition between incumbent and opposing elites, between incumbent elites and special interests, among ethnic groups (black vs. blacks, blacks vs. Arabs or arabized, or black vs. such other groups as Indians or Lebanese), and among "racial" groups. (This latter term is used to denote political control by whites rather than cases where black or arabized minorities control "racially" distinct majorities.)

The second pattern involves inter-African conflicts, which tend to be seen as personal, ideological, and/or territorial. Personal antagonisms among African leaders abound; they derive their import not from any intrinsic feature, but from the fact that leaders tend to monopolize the definition and control of their states' foreign relations. In time, foreign policy may become institutionalized and the importance of personal factors will decline accordingly. The same generalization can be made about ideological conflicts. Territorial issues concern border disputes, irredentism, and/or competition for scarce resources located astride or beyond existing political boundaries. The energy with which these territorial issues are pursued, however, is considerably limited by the realization that boundaries, "artificial" though they are, are best maintained intact. To base them on such natural criteria as traditional ethnic or religious, or modern economic/rational, may be either ludicrous or dangerous or both.

9

The third general conflict pattern in African foreign policy relates to conflicts among powerful outside forces and their repercussions in Africa. Such issues refer chiefly to the period of the intensely ideological cold war, but they can also be applied to larger international economic relationships and to questions of the new north/south division between rich and poor countries. Such conflicts in Africa were never intense or widespread. Occasionally African states invited support from one side or the other in the cold war, but without much success. Among external influences in Africa, those of Western powers, particularly Western Europe, are still predominant. Russian and Chinese efforts to influence Africa have often been exaggerated by Western observers; efforts by Arab Middle Eastern states have begun only recently. One of the ironies of the demise of the cold war was that it deprived Africans of a number of foreign relations levers.

I.W. Zartman suggests that the chief determinant of the foreign relations of African states is neither sovereignty nor power, but ideology. Since many African states use concepts larger than state sovereignty in order to seek to alter other states' domestic and foreign policies—not only in southern Africa—it is evident that the notion of state sovereignty is not always their major practical concern. The tools used most frequently include propaganda, subversion, threats, conspiracies, guerilla warfare, and occasional limited conventional warfare (the latter instrument normally reserved for anti-colonialism). Moreover, power as a concept is rarely used in African foreign policy. The reason seems evident. Their power, as measured by traditional standards, is benign or nonexistent. But since power is a relational concept, and since there are occasional but significant power disparities among African states, reluctance to think in terms of power needs to be accounted for in other ways. The answer may lie in one aspect of ideology: "Because African leaders succeeded in crumbling the walls of the major world empires by blowing on ideological trumpets and parading around the citadels of colonialism, there is a continuing tendency to believe in the power of slogans and ideas" (Zartman, NEW AFRICA, p. 55).

The importance of ideology in this context can be traced to several factors. In addition to fostering myths based on past experience, ideology serves as a building bloc for national unity, and leaders' ideological pronouncements on foreign policy issues are often revered as gospel. Furthermore, the world of international relations, from whose direct political control these have but recently emerged, is based on the use of power. Since the new states do not currently hold such power, they tend to reject such assumptions about international relations and to construct ideological alternatives which exclude power. The new world requires the "creation and acceptance of a new system of values that denigrates power. . . . Because the existence of power . . . cannot be denied, it must be disarmed" (Zartman, NEW AFRICA, p. 145). It is not surprising, therefore, that foreign policy at times takes on an unyielding quality, a puritanical devotion to visions of the future which may (as has often been observed) bear little relation to national interests as defined in other ways.

10

In addition to foreign policy, some writers have focused on inter-African diplomatic ties from the perspective of their "normalization," somewhat ambiguously defined quantitatively as a "pattern of diplomatic activity such that . . . proper emphasis is given to relations with neighbours, and with regional and continentally powerful states," proper emphasis presumably meaning the existence of reciprocal diplomatic ties (Johns, "Normalization," p. 598). A quantitative definition of what is normal, however, leaves a number of important questions unanswered. If the criterion for diplomatic ties were some concrete benefit, there would be little reason to blanket the continent with resident or other accredited diplomatic missions. Were one to look at motivations, one would find overlapping sets of criteria much closer to reality. Such a list would include personal ties among political leaders; actual or potential economic benefits; religious ties; cultural affinities; simple maintenance of existing ties; and political considerations including prestige, the preferences of host countries, nonalignment, extension of influence abroad, the attraction of other states' social experiments, suspicion of other states, a desire for listening posts, special relations with contiguous states, and promises made by host countries. Normalcy defined as the maximum possible number of diplomatic ties seems excessive, since for reasons of interest and finances, African states are eclective in sending diplomatic missions abroad.

Finally, it is often overlooked that the foreign policy of African states tends to be revisionist, in the sense that the states are committed to changing basic aspects of the present international system. Domestic social, economic, and political problems and the external condition of comparative poverty support African demands for a more equitable distribution of rewards at the global level. It is essential that foreign, particularly Western observers take this into account, if only because of their tendency to assume moderation, stability, and orderly progress as a universal norm of international relations.

B. GENERAL INTERNATIONAL RELATIONS

1   Bell, J. Bowyer. THE HORN OF AFRICA: STRATEGIC MAGNET IN THE SEVENTIES. New York: National Strategy Information Center, 1973. 49 p. Bibliography.

A short introduction to some strategic problems in that area, seen mostly as a function of geography, but complicated by indigenous and historically rooted frictions which are aggravated by external involvement--Arab, Israeli, Russian, Chinese, and American, all potentially serious. The area's importance is likely to grow in the future.

2   Brooks, Hugh C., and el-Ayouti, Yassin, eds. REFUGEES SOUTH OF THE SAHARA: AN AFRICAN DILEMMA. Westport, Conn.: Negro Universities Press, 1970. 291 p. Appendices, index.

A stark report if only by virtue of the number and distribution of refugees--there are more than one million (in 1967, more than 900,000: nearly one-half from white-dominated regions, 300,000 from Angola, 120,000 from Rwanda, 70,000 Somalis in Ethiopia, and about 65,000 from Guinea-Bissau in Senegal). The book probes the background and the motives (growth of restrictive nationalism, tribal and frontier problems, jobs, political unrest). It also covers legal considerations, the effect on states, the uses made of refugees, American and United Nations aid, and case studies (the Sudan, the French Territory of the Afar and Issa, Portuguese Guinea, southern Africa, Zaire, and South West Africa). Contributors point out that refugees come from black-ruled and white-ruled states; they create problems for the host countries, many of which are among the world's poorest. They are assisted by the United Nations and some eighty private organizations (a list is appended).

3   Cesaire, Aime. DISCOURSE ON COLONIALISM. Translated by Joan Pinkham. New York: Monthly Review, 1972. 79 p.

An indictment of the influence of European values and behavior, extending in time from pre-World War I ferment and in scope to the Third World. It traces the influence of colonization, Christianity, science, and communism. The Martiniquan writer chronicles black people's revolt against colonial hypocrisy and the alienation it engendered.

4   Cottrell, Alvin J., and Burrell, R.M., eds. THE INDIAN OCEAN: ITS POLITICAL, ECONOMIC, AND MILITARY IMPORTANCE. New York: Praeger, for the Center for Strategic and International Studies, Georgetown University, 1972. 433 p. Tables, maps.

A basic study of international aspects of the area surrounding the Indian Ocean. The book contains essays on the competition for power in the African Horn, on Ethiopia, southern and South Africa, and the islands, including Madagascar. Another section discusses interests and policies in that area of Russia, the People's Republic of China, Western Europe, Great Britain, and the United States, in addition to relations with countries in other parts of Asia and the Middle East. Contributions are by well known specialists.

5   Cowan, L. Gray. BLACK AFRICA: THE GROWING PAINS OF INDEPENDENCE. Headline Series, no. 210. New York: Foreign Policy Association, April 1972. 60 p. Paperback.

Review of major political, economic, and social developments in Africa since independence, with brief discussions of relations with the world and of American policy.

6   _____. THE DILEMMAS OF AFRICAN INDEPENDENCE. Rev. ed.

New York: Walker, 1968.   158 p.   Bibliography.

Introductory essays on nationalism, economic problems, and the new states' foreign policy.   Part two is a compilation of basic data for reference on society, culture, land, and resources, and brief sketches of inter-African institutions.

7   Crocker, Chester A.   "External Military Assistance to Africa."   AFRICA TODAY 15 (April-May 1968):   15-20.

A brief study which finds that, although Africa is of no great strategic and military concern to external powers and spends comparatively little on defense, military aid is nonetheless important to recipient states because of the domestic role of their armed forces and the potential for escalation of civil and border conflicts, particularly in the Horn and in southern Africa.   The essay includes a discussion of aid policies of Great Britain, France, West Germany, the United States, the Communist countries, and other sources.

8   Dumoga, John.   AFRICA BETWEEN EAST AND WEST.   Chester Springs, Pa.:   Dufour Editions, 1969.   131 p.

A useful review of select aspects of the foreign policy behavior of African states, emphasizing the former British colonies. The author believes that external influences, though potent, are not compelling in Africa, and he urges that political leaders be more tolerant of dissenters.

9   Ferkiss, Victor.   AFRICA'S SEARCH FOR IDENTITY.   New York: Braziller, 1966.   340 p.

A general introduction to Africa by a sympathetic observer. After giving some background, the author discusses Africa's emerging relations within Africa and with Europe, the Third World, the socialist states, and the United States.   Ferkiss contends that Africa is a released captive rather than a child growing up; along with some African intellectuals and Teilhard de Chardin, the writer suggests that Africa needs to contribute to world civilization to become a full-fledged member of the world community.

10   Green, Reginald H., and Seidman, Ann.   UNITY OR POVERTY?   THE ECONOMICS OF PAN-AFRICANISM.   Baltimore: Penguin, 1968. 352 p.   Paperback.

An overview of African economic problems from the vantage point of a profound commitment to unification.   The authors end with a plea for political unity to bring about more rational economic activity and growth to stand up to external forces.

11   Kamarck, Andrew M. THE ECONOMICS OF AFRICAN DEVELOPMENT.
      Rev. ed. New York: Praeger, 1971. 340 p. Maps, tables, appen-
      dices.

      A survey of the background, structure, impediments to, and
      opportunities for economic development. Separate chapters
      treat the colonial impact, Africa's economy in relation to the
      world, agriculture, industry, infrastructure, foreign aid and
      investment, planning, diplomacy, and future prospects.

12   Kesteloot, Lilyan. INTELLECTUAL ORIGINS OF THE AFRICAN REVO-
      LUTION. Washington, D.C.: Black Orpheus, 1972. 113 p.

      A highly provocative look at antecedents to the era of political
      independence, with emphasis on African intellectuals' contribu-
      tions. The author sees European control over Africa as ending
      largely because of African intellectuals' demands for eventual
      independence in the 1920s and the crumbling myths of European
      dominance that supported colonialism, leading to an inevitable
      rebirth of awareness of and faith in a resilient African culture
      and civilization. The author challenges the criticism that Af-
      ricans have idealized their past or become racists and suggests
      that instead they advocate retaining some traditions and adap-
      ting others to modernization.

13   McKay, Vernon. AFRICA IN WORLD POLITICS. New York: Harper
      & Row, 1963. 425 p. Tables.

      A pioneering effort and useful source for any review of Africa
      and the world. Part 1 discusses relations in and with the
      United Nations; part 2, pan-Africanism and ties with Europe;
      part 3, relations with India and the Soviet Union; and part 4,
      relations with the United States, including a detailed review
      of the genesis of U.S. policy. Some of the information and per-
      ceptions are necessarily dated; however, the book provides es-
      sential background.

14   Marvin, David K., ed. EMERGING AFRICA IN WORLD AFFAIRS.
      San Francisco: Chandler, 1965. 311 p. Paperback.

      A collection of forty-two essays in four parts under the head-
      ings of colonialism, African unity, external economic ties, and
      Africa in world politics. Of particular interest are discussions
      of neutralism and the mix of African, European, and American
      authors selected. The book presents good background for the
      novice.

15   Mazrui, Ali A. TOWARDS A PAX AFRICANA: A STUDY OF IDEOL-
      OGY AND AMBITION. Chicago: University of Chicago Press, 1967.
      216 p. Appendices.

Pan-Africanism, Unity, and Foreign Policy

A stimulating collection of essays on diverse topics with central
or tangential relevance for students of international affairs.
They are grouped into two sections, one on ideology and identity and another on dilemmas of statehood. The chapter entitled "On the Concept of 'We Are All Africans'" and the one
conceptualizing the "Pax Africana" are among the most provocative. The appendices include the text of the charter of the
OAU and the first resolutions adopted by that organization.

16   Miller, J.D.B. THE POLITICS OF THE THIRD WORLD. New York:
     Oxford University Press, 1967. 126 p. Paperback.

     A short, impressionistic, and cogent treatment of Third World
     international behavior, emphasizing the many western miscon-
     ceptions about that subject. There are separate discussions of
     background, and of relations with the major powers and the
     UN, and among Third World countries.

17   Moraes, Frank. THE IMPORTANCE OF BEING BLACK: AN ASIAN
     LOOKS AT AFRICA. Bibliography of Indian Publications on Africa.
     New York: Macmillan; London: Collier-Macmillan, 1965. 413 p.

     An Indian newspaperman and editor's impressions during a four-
     month visit to Africa. What the book lacks in depth, its nar-
     rative makes up for in keenness of observation, particularly
     about the rootlessness of Africa after the colonial experience.
     Hence to be black (or white in South Africa) is important, but
     in ways which are not entirely clear.

18   Nielsen, Waldemar A. THE GREAT POWERS AND AFRICA. New York:
     Praeger, for the Council on Foreign Relations, 1969. 404 p. Tables.

     The most comprehensive, most useful treatment of the subject.
     Part 1 is about Europe, part 2 the Communist states (Russia and
     China), and parts 3 and 4 the United States and Africa. The
     style is flowing, and language is used skillfully, so much so
     that only a careful reading yields what is really being said.
     The author's sympathies lie with African self-determination, but
     he places a high premium on stability. His policy recommenda-
     tions demonstrate the ambiguities inherent in American relations
     with Africa.

19   Padelford, Norman J., and Emerson, Rupert, eds. AFRICA AND WORLD
     ORDER. New York: Praeger, 1966. 136 p. Bibliography, paperback.

     A collection of seven essays, one on pan-Africanism; one on
     the Commonwealth; four on the United Nations; and one a de-
     scription of the complex unification movements in Africa. The
     first essay is by Rupert Emerson; the others are by generalists.

15

20   Quaison-Sackey, Alex. AFRICA UNBOUND: REFLECTIONS OF AN
      AFRICAN STATESMAN. New York: Praeger, 1963. 174 p. Paper-
      back.

      Personalized, articulate discussions of the movement toward in-
      dependence, the concepts of the African personality and neu-
      tralism, the United Nations, and reminiscences by a Ghanaian
      delegate to the United Nations. Much of it reads like an
      apologia for Kwame Nkrumah, as well as an optimistic state-
      ment of Africa's self-assertion in the world.

21   Quigg, Philip W., ed. AFRICA: A FOREIGN AFFAIRS READER.
      New York: Praeger, for the Council on Foreign Relations, 1964. 338 p.

      A selection of twenty-four articles published in FOREIGN AF-
      FAIRS between 1926 and 1963. Written by Africans, Americans,
      and Europeans, these articles cover such topics as colonialism
      and the development of self-government, South Africa, African
      "isms," and essays by African leaders. They were selected to
      emphasize differing conceptions about major issues, and most
      are worth rereading.

22   Rivkin, Arnold. THE AFRICAN PRESENCE IN WORLD AFFAIRS: NA-
      TIONAL DEVELOPMENT AND ITS ROLE IN FOREIGN POLICY. New
      York: Free Press, for the Center for International Studies, Massachusetts
      Institute of Technology, 1963. 262 p.

      An examination of some of the domestic determinants of the
      new states' foreign policy behavior. It assumes that political
      stability is the major precondition for further economic develop-
      ment and thus emphasizes ways used to consolidate power. The
      criteria used are at times based on Western notions, such as
      ideology for "left authoritarian" regimes and pragmatic domes-
      tic needs for "right authoritarian" systems. Part 2 is a useful
      review of problems of economic growth, and part 3 focuses on
      nationalism and its relation to unity and ties with Europe, as
      well as on African behavior at the United Nations. The au-
      thor suggests that the United States ought to base its policy
      not on ideology but on American national interest.

23   Said, Abdul A. THE AFRICAN PHENOMENON. Boston: Allyn and
      Bacon, 1968. 158 p. Appendices, paperback.

      A sound primer which includes the ambivalent nature of African
      political and social thought. It also reviews the meaning of
      nationalism, socialism, pan-Africanism, and neutralism, as
      expressions of freedom, progress, order, and security, respec-
      tively. The introduction contains a provocative discussion of
      western scholars' efforts to come to grips with the nonwestern
      world. Main chapters discuss the thoughts of representative
      African political leaders.

24   "South Africa." In THE ARMS TRADE WITH THE THIRD WORLD,
      pp. 675-84. Stockholm: Stockholm International Peace Research Insti-
      tute, 1971.

      A brief review of the arms buildup in that country, which ex-
      plains why the arms embargo has not been successful.

25   Streeten, Paul. AID TO AFRICA: A POLICY OUTLINE FOR THE
      1970's. New York: Praeger, 1972. 169 p. Tables, charts.

      A study commissioned by the United Nations Economic Com-
      mission for Africa. Fifteen chapters review donor countries'
      policies, trends in assistance flows, priorities, and special as-
      pects of international economic aid such as debt servicing,
      planning and coordination, and "tying." A brief chapter on
      the special claims of Africa rests on the question of their need
      and argues that inequities should be removed. Statistical tables
      are outdated, apparently based on United Nations rather than
      national statistics.

26   "Sub-Sahara Africa." In THE ARMS TRADE WITH THE THIRD WORLD,
      pp. 597-674. Stockholm: Stockholm International Peace Research Insti-
      tute, 1971.

      Statistical data on weapons acquisitions between 1950 and 1969,
      accompanied by discussions of factors affecting demand and the
      role of suppliers (the pattern differs from the global one). Spe-
      cific attention is given to individual states and to African
      liberation movements.

27   Widstrand, Carl Goesta, ed. AFRICAN BOUNDARY PROBLEMS. Up-
      psala: Scandinavian Institute of African Studies, 1969. 183 p. Ap-
      pendices, paperback.

      A review by ten specialists of problems related to the study of
      boundaries; legal, economic, irredentist, and foreign policy
      factors involved; colonial determinants; positions taken by the
      Organization of African Unity; and the frontiers of southern
      Africa. The relationship between historical and political claims
      for territory are not clear, but natural resources have played
      an important part in generating such demands.

28   Zartman, I. William. THE SAHARA--BRIDGE OR BARRIER? New York:
      International Conciliation, no. 541, 1963. 60 p. Paperback.

      An examination, after a review of pertinent background, of
      French efforts at interstate cooperation and on the Maghreb
      with emphasis on Moroccan irredentism and the Casablanca
      Group. The author suggests that the desert need not be a
      barrier to cooperation, but that cooperative efforts are only in
      their infancy.

C. UNITY AND PAN-AFRICANISM

29   Andemicael, Berhanykun. PEACEFUL SETTLEMENT AMONG AFRICAN
STATES: ROLES OF THE UNITED NATIONS AND THE ORGANIZATION
OF AFRICAN UNITY. New York: United Nations Institute for Training
and Research, 1972. 54 p. Bibliography, paperback.

An examination of the relations between the two international
organizations, done mainly by distinguishing conflicts arising
from domestic tensions from those having external roots. Although the OAU charter contains little on relations with the
United Nations, that question arises in practice. Since the
OAU has attempted to be an instrument of the first instance,
the United Nations has played a residual role. The OAU is
more effective in creating conditions to normalize African interstate relations than in settling conflict.

30   Arkhurst, Frederick S., ed. AFRICA IN THE SEVENTIES AND EIGHTIES:
ISSUES IN DEVELOPMENT. New York: Praeger, in cooperation with
the Adlai Stevenson Institute of International Affairs, 1970. 400 p.
Tables, statistical appendix.

Contributions providing useful background on such topics as
political, social, administrative, economic, and legal developments. Chapter 2 reviews Africa's external trade, and chapter
12 the prospects for inter-African economic integration.

31   Boutros-Ghali, Boutros. THE ADDIS ABABA CHARTER. International
Conciliation Series, no. 546. New York: International Conciliation,
1964. 62 p. Paperback.

An early, chiefly descriptive look at the document that created
the OAU, and at the various organs mentioned in the charter.

32   Bowman, Larry W. "The Subordinate System of Southern Africa." INTER-
NATIONAL STUDIES QUARTERLY 12 (September 1968): 231-61.

An attempt to move beyond discrete analysis of individual actors, racial foci, or constitutional developments by positing an
international subsystem set apart by internal interaction and to
abstract solidity from economic, political, and social ties.
The criteria used include geographic scope, number of units,
identification, and relation to the dominant system (in this
case the major powers). The subsystem is characterized by
South African dominance, the growth of interaction, and by
its relative behavioral independence from the major powers.
The system is also found to be stable, a factor which tends to
enhance world stability.

33   Cervenka, Zdenek. THE ORGANIZATION OF UNITY AND ITS

CHARTER. New York: Praeger, 1969. 248 p. Appendices.

A primarily legalistic presentation of the creation and early operation of the OAU, plus discussions of the relations between that organization and African regional groups, the 1965 crisis about Rhodesia, and the Nigerian civil war. He suggests that, despite many shortcomings, African leaders will strengthen the organization.

34   Currie, David P., ed. FEDERALISM AND THE NEW NATIONS OF AFRICA. Chicago: University of Chicago Press; Toronto: University of Toronto Press, 1964. 436 p.

A record of sixteen papers and attendant discussion at a 1962 symposium held at the Center for Legal Research of the University of Chicago Law School. The papers focus on four interrelated subjects. The first is history in the east, central, former French west, and former British west Africa, and in the United States. The other three focus on the relationship between economic growth, human rights, and international law.

35   Farajallah, Samaan Boutros. LE GROUPE AFRO-ASIATIQUE DANS LES NATIONS UNIES. Geneva: Droz, 1963. 457 p. Bibliography, paperback.

A review of the creation and structure of the Afro-Asian group, in and outside the United Nations, followed by case studies focusing on objectives, techniques, and cohesion. The author finds that the group's motives are anchored in the component states' individual national interests and concludes that the group is bound to become fragmented. The group's effective cohesion differed widely as a function of general or specific questions, and the author foresees the gradual erosion of African (and Asian) countries' ties with former metropolitan powers.

36   Hazlewood, Arthur, ed. AFRICAN INTEGRATION AND DISINTEGRATION: CASE STUDIES IN ECONOMIC AND POLITICAL UNION. London: Oxford University Press, 1967. 394 p. Appendix.

A selective collection of essays divided into economic, political, and wider unification schemes. The essays provide useful background, reflect on the meager success of unity in Africa, and suggest that African leaders have become more attuned to reality than they were in the flush of independence.

37   Hovet, Thomas, Jr. AFRICA IN THE UNITED NATIONS. Evanston, Ill.: Northwestern University Press, 1963. 326 p. Tables, charts, appendices, index.

A thorough examination of African states' roll call votes in plenary sessions of the General Assembly between 1946 and

1962, with emphasis on interpreting these votes (which are not
necessarily representative of national policy) in light of Africa's
impact on the UN. After discussing cohesion, factions, and
impact, the author suggests that Africa's main impact was more
potential than actual; it can raise moral issues, can control the
Economic and Social Council and the Trusteeship Council, and
can increase its overall negotiating potential.

38   Hughes, A.J. EAST AFRICA: THE SEARCH FOR UNITY. Baltimore:
      Penguin, 1963. 264 p. Appendix, paperback.

      A convenient history of the background influences on and
      political developments in Tanganyika, Kenya, Uganda, and
      Zanzibar, followed by a review of efforts toward an east Afri-
      can federation. Written at a time when prospects looked hope-
      ful, by a sympathetic observer.

39   Kapungu, Leonard T. THE UNITED NATIONS AND ECONOMIC SANC-
      TIONS AGAINST RHODESIA. Lexington, Mass.: Heath, 1971. 141 p.
      Maps, charts.

      A labored account of Rhodesia's independence and of the prob-
      lems related to UN sanctions. It is useful as background read-
      ing.

40   Keatley, Patrick. THE POLITICS OF PARTNERSHIP: THE FEDERATION
      OF RHODESIA AND NYASALAND. Baltimore: Penguin, 1963. 505 p.
      Appendix, maps, paperback.

      A lively review of the evolution of one of the last attempts by
      British settlers, in what is now Malawi, Zambia, and Rhodesia,
      to maintain their dominant position. The author suggests that
      on moral and practical grounds, the British government should
      encourage the settlers in accepting the African revolution.

41   Legum, Colin. PAN-AFRICANISM: A SHORT POLITICAL GUIDE.
      Rev. ed. New York: Praeger, 1965. 308 p. Appendices, documents
      (pp. 151-308), paperback.

      A solid, basic introduction which reviews the roots and growth
      of the concept and its adoption within Africa and interprets
      inter-African unification efforts between 1958 and 1962 in that
      light. It includes chapters on African workers, on connections
      between politics and culture, and on political thought. The
      text is well written and makes liberal use of quotations. A
      collection of documents in the appendix (pp. 151-308) is useful
      for basic research.

42   Marquard, Leo. A FEDERATION OF SOUTHERN AFRICA. London:
      Oxford University Press, 1971. 139 p. Index.

A cool-headed discussion emphasizing rational, constitutional, legal, structural, and electoral facets and addressing both advantages and disadvantages of this hypothetical possibility. It would provide an alternative to existing arrangements and would avoid supremacy by any racial group and engender or facilitate peaceful coexistence, provided that whites altered their present perceptions and saw the wisdom of sharing, rather than monopolizing or abandoning, political power.

43   Meyers, B. David. "Intraregional Conflict Management by the Organization of African Unity." INTERNATIONAL ORGANIZATION 28 (Summer 1974): 345-73.

A discussion of the major limitations and restricted authority of the OAU in this field. After reviewing a number of cases of conflict management differentiated by categories, the writer concludes that the OAU can propitiate and help settlement rather than direct it and that intra-African authority is heavily fragmented.

44   Mushkat, Marion. "Problems of Political and Organizational Unity in Africa." AFRICAN STUDIES REVIEW 13 (September 1970): 269-90.

A review article on historical, political, economic, and structural elements of the Organization of African Unity. It discusses the OAU's most significant successes and shortcomings and suggests that the organization, although it is African, is an example of a more universal phenomenon. The assessment of the OAU's ability and/or readiness to keep external influences at bay, to the extent that it is based upon long-time resistance to Arab overtures with respect to Israel, needs to be reconsidered, perhaps by distinguishing African perceptions of desirable and undesirable outside involvement.

45   Mutharika, B.W.T. TOWARD MULTINATIONAL ECONOMIC COOPERATION IN AFRICA. New York: Praeger, 1972. 391 p. Tables, appendix, bibliography.

A detailed survey of the chances and realities of increasing inter-African economic ties. Part 1 reviews the framework and various approaches; part 2 suggests a plan for greater integration in trade, industry, and communications; and part 3 reviews achievements and constraints of the first decade of independence. The conclusion calls for greater realism in respecting economic factors.

46   Potholm, Christian P., and Dale, Richard, eds. SOUTHERN AFRICA IN PERSPECTIVE: ESSAYS IN REGIONAL POLITICS. New York: Free Press; London: Collier-Macmillan, 1972. 331 p. Index.

0505191

The editors identify four major shortcomings in the literature,
to which this collection is addressed: the lack of balanced
presentation, of dispassionate works, of up-to-date materials,
and of systemic analysis for the region. They achieved this
objective on the first three (one could question the balance),
and made a step forward regarding the fourth. Four substantive
parts follow, each divided into "country profiles" which follow
colonial divisions or are presented as "influence vectors." Part 6
covers relations with the Organization of African Unity, military factors, a sensitive, candid assessment of the exile condition, and regional integration. A strength of the volume is
that it enables the reader to pursue systemic analysis beyond
that provided in a few of the contributions.

47   Rothchild, Donald S. TOWARD UNITY IN AFRICA: A STUDY OF
      FEDERALISM IN EAST AFRICA. Washington, D.C.: Public Affairs Press,
      1960. 193 p.

      An examination of attempts at federation among African states,
      with emphasis on East Africa, Rhodesia and Nyasaland, and
      west Africa.

48   Skurnik, W.A.E. "Senghor on Culture: The African and International
      Contexts." AFRICAN FORUM 3 (Fall 1967 and Winter 1968): 25-43.

      An exploration of the cultural theories of the architect of
      Senegal's foreign relations, which tend toward cross-pollination
      in a pluralistic world. The foundations of that thought and its
      effects on policy are traced. President Senghor is seen not only
      as an influential intellectual but also as a man of high ideals
      and a representative of moderation in African foreign policy.

49   Tevoedjre, Albert. PAN-AFRICANISM IN ACTION: AN ACCOUNT OF
      THE UAM. Occasional Paper no. 11. Cambridge, Mass.: Harvard
      University Press, Center for International Affairs, November 1965. 86 p.
      Paperback.

      A brief but competent narrative account of the Union Africaine
      et Malgache by its former secretary-general. The book focuses
      on background, structures, and two case studies. The interpre-
      tation reflects the intellectual convictions and ambiguities of
      some African leaders in the 1960s.

50   Thompson, Virginia. WEST AFRICA'S COUNCIL OF THE ENTENTE.
      Ithaca, N.Y.: Cornell University Press, 1972. 286 p. Bibliography,
      charts, illustrations.

      A comprehensive study of the only west African unity effort that
      achieved some measure of success by a longtime student of for-
      mer French black Africa. The entente is nonetheless seen as
      fragile and perhaps unable to survive the leadership of Ivory

Coast President Felix Houphouet-Boigny.

51   Thompson, W. Scott, and Bissell, Richard. "Legitimacy and Authority in the OAU." AFRICAN STUDIES REVIEW 15 (April 1972): 17-42.

An article concerning whether or not African unity is a myth. It addresses the question whether its institutional embodiment, the OAU, is coping with problems by focusing on the concepts of legitimacy and authority. The authors conclude that the OAU has weakened since its promising beginning.

52   Wallerstein, Immanuel. AFRICA: THE POLITICS OF UNITY. New York: Random House, 1967. 253 p. Appendices.

A highly readable account of unification efforts, inspired more by ideological commitment than by the actual behavior of most African states. The author uses the notions of a core of revolutionary states, dedicated to the unity of the people and to the transformation of Africa and the world and of a periphery, pursuing narrow national interests and playing the game. The book attributes the failure of the core to move the periphery in the right direction to external forces.

53   Welch, Claude E., Jr. DREAM OF UNITY: PAN-AFRICANISM AND POLITICAL UNIFICATION IN WEST AFRICA. Ithaca, N.Y.: Cornell University Press, 1966. 361 p. Maps, tables, bibliography.

A review of unification attempts among the Ewe, in the Cameroons, between Senegal and the Gambia, and of the Ghana-Guinea-Mali Union. Also discussed are three types of unity in the African context. Welch points out that unification is more difficult after independence than before, and he gives consideration to pan-Africanism. The last chapter addresses some theoretical notions and questions of elite behavior.

54   Woronoff, Jon. ORGANIZING AFRICAN UNITY. Metuchen, N.J.: Scarecrow Press, 1970. 639 p. Annexes.

A major study of unity efforts by a close observer. The discussion is broken down into the genesis of pan-Africanism; creation of the Organization of African Unity; and problems related to decolonization, domestic order, nonalignment, economic growth, and regionalism. The conclusion states that the mystique of unity in Africa has faded and calls for realism and courage on the part of African leaders.

55   Zartman, I. William. INTERNATIONAL RELATIONS IN THE NEW AFRICA. Englewood Cliffs, N.J.: Prentice Hall, 1966. 166 p. Paperback.

A seminal study which discusses preindependence international

89313

relations, the difficult and confused task of defining national
interests, and the limits operating on inter-African relations.
The book is both theoretical and well-documented. Zartman
sees the drive for unity as a defensive reaction against real
and imagined external threats, and suggests that existing patterns are likely to endure.

D. FOREIGN POLICY AND DIPLOMACY

56   Aynor, H.S. NOTES FROM AFRICA. New York: Praeger, 1969.
      163 p.

      A sensitive and sympathetic comment on sub-Saharan Africa
      written by an Israeli foreign service official and former ambas-
      sador in west Africa. Aynor criticizes government and intel-
      lectual elites for excessive formalism and sometime lack of
      dedication. His discussion of differences and similarities be-
      tween French and British influences is extremely worthwhile.
      The book, which is in the form of a hypothetical diary, calls
      for drastic changes if economic growth is to be achieved.

57   Barber, James. SOUTH AFRICA'S FOREIGN POLICY, 1945-1970. Lon-
      don: Oxford University Press, 1973. 308 p. Tables, maps, illustrations.

      A cumbersomely written but valuable book with an essential
      grasp of the determinants and objectives of the country's foreign
      policy and a hard-headed view of international, and particularly
      British, realities. South African foreign relations emerge as
      more flexible than frozen, but they seem aimed at a defensive
      posture dominated by the main objective of continued white
      supremacy.

58   Brown, Douglas. AGAINST THE WORLD: ATTITUDES OF WHITE SOUTH
      AFRICA. Garden City, N.Y.: Doubleday, 1969. 253 p. Paperback.

      An inquiry into the roots of white supremacy and the resulting
      racial tensions with consideration of such topics as political
      institutions, economic wealth, customs, and religious beliefs.
      The author faults both the South African government for refusing
      to adjust to evolving reality and external critics for acting on
      the bases of ignorance and absolute commitment.

59   Brown, Irene. "Studies in Non-Alignment." JOURNAL OF MODERN
      AFRICAN STUDIES 4 (December 1966): 517-27.

      A discussion based chiefly on two books, one by Crabb and the
      other by Jansen (cited below). The author shows that nonalign-
      ment is now an important part of the international relations be-
      havior which began with the creation of the UN. She views
      nonalignment within the context of the cold war and urges the

superpowers to shed stereotyped preconceptions about developing countries.

60   Carroll, Faye. SOUTH WEST AFRICA AND THE UNITED NATIONS. Lexington: University of Kentucky Press, 1967. 113 p. Appendix.

A competent discussion of a vexing question. Although none of the UN objectives were completely achieved, UN involvement has defined the territory's status legally, added to South Africa's isolation in the world, and prevented South Africa from totally annexing South West Africa.

61   Crabb, Cecil V., ed. THE ELEPHANTS AND THE GRASS: A STUDY OF NON-ALIGNMENT. New York: Praeger, 1965. 237 p.

A primer on a confusing topic. The book begins by examining properties of the concept and its genesis, then turns to nonalignment "policies" and orientation concerning the international state system and the United Nations, and then considers relations with the Communist bloc and the United States. The nonalignment movement is viewed as flexible and therefore successful in some of its objectives. It also has benefited from the incipient demise of the cold war, particularly from the consequences of technological advances in weapons systems which undercut the need for allies among Third World states. The author suggests that nonalignment is a sound doctrine which serves national interests of its adherents and that it is likely to be a permanent feature of the world system.

62   Dale, Richard. BOTSWANA AND ITS SOUTHERN NEIGHBOR: THE PATTERNS OF LINKAGE AND THE OPTIONS IN STATECRAFT. Paper in International Studies, Africa Series no. 6. Athens: Ohio University Center for International Studies, 1970. 22 p. Paperback.

A challenge to the conventional view that Botswana is entirely dominated by South Africa. It shows that South Africa is confused about policy toward its northern neighbor, that Botswana can make skillful use of bargaining to avoid being a client state in a number of inter-African and extra-African issue areas, and that it can influence some elements of South African domestic and foreign policy.

63   Forsyth, Frederick. THE BIAFRA STORY. Baltimore: Penguin, 1969. 235 p. Paperback.

A colorful, pro-Biafran account of what is today called the Nigerian civil war, with provocative views about the role of external African and extra-African powers.

64   Gerard-Libois, Jules. KATANGA SECESSION. Translated by Rebecca

Young. Madison: University of Wisconsin Press, 1966. 289 p. Appendix.

Essentially an account of relations between Katanga and the Congo, but the author points out the inextricable links with the policies of Belgium and the United Nations. The emphasis is on events inside Katanga before and during its secession between 1960 and 1963.

65   Hall, Richard. THE HIGH PRICE OF PRINCIPLES: KAUNDA AND THE WHITE SOUTH. New York: Africana, 1969. 248 p. Index.

An account of developments in Zambia, the only country in southern Africa which, after its political independence, consciously drew away from the South and laid the foundations for a basic reorientation of her external relations. This book is a chatty, and highly sympathetic, account of that reorientation under the leadership of President Kaunda, despite considerable pressures and difficulties.

66   Hoskyns, Catherine, ed. THE ETHIOPIA-SOMALIA-KENYA DISPUTE, 1960-1967. Dar es Salaam: Oxford University Press, for the Institute of Public Administration, University College, Dar es Salaam, 1969. 90 p. Tables, paperback.

A useful historical model for the study of inter-African conflict. In addition to a collection of documents and comments on the issue discussed, the author provides a background sketch and a chronology of events.

67   Idang, Gordon J. NIGERIA: INTERNAL POLITICS AND FOREIGN POLICY (1960-1966). Ibadan, Nigeria: Ibadan University Press, 1974. 160 p. Select bibliography, paperback.

A study about Nigeria under Premier Balewa. In few African countries is it possible to identify, much less relate, domestic to external determinants of foreign policy behavior; the absence of clear public opinion, the fragility of bureaucratic organizations, rapidly changing societies, and the room left for leaders' idiosyncracies all work against systematic analysis. This study explores three areas: (1) official statements, elements of ideology, and the general domestic context; (2) the views of elites, parties, public opinion, and the media; (3) foreign policy substance and implementation. The treatment of data is competent; the conclusions drawn, however, are unnecessarily impressionistic.

68   Ismael, Tarek Y. THE U.A.R. IN AFRICA: EGYPT'S POLICY UNDER NASSER. Evanston, Ill.: Northwestern University Press, 1971. 233 p. Maps, appendices.

A candid historical account of the motives, development, and objectives of Egypt's policy under Nasser, complemented by case studies of the Sudan and the Congo. The account is, on the balance, unfavorable; it also contains little systematic analysis and leaves unclear a number of assertions.

69   Jansen, G.H. NONALIGNMENT AND THE AFRO-ASIAN STATES. New York: Praeger, 1966. 407 p. Appendices.

A detailed review of the evolution of the Afro-Asian bloc. The author, an Indian foreign correspondent, highlights three themes operating within the bloc: the importance attached to morality in international affairs, nonalignment, and the gap between fact and desire. He suggests that the group will continue to fragment and that national interests will reassert themselves.

70   Johns, David H. "The 'Normalization' of Inter-African Diplomatic Activity." JOURNAL OF MODERN AFRICAN STUDIES 10 (December 1972): 597–610.

An examination of formal inter-African diplomatic ties (sending diplomats, establishing missions) since independence. Johns highlights patterns of greatest and weakest intensity (greatest in coastal, western, former French, and moderate states) and suggests that normalization or existence of such ties may be a sign of African unity.

71   McGowan, Patrick J. "Africa and Non-Alignment: A Comparative Study of Foreign Policy." INTERNATIONAL STUDIES QUARTERLY 12 (September 1968): 262–92.

An excursion into the measurement of alignment, or interaction with Communist states, using the notion of James Rosenau's pre-theory and applying factor and correlational analysis to show patterns of behavior and to suggest a number of hypotheses for replication.

72   McKay, Vernon, ed. AFRICAN DIPLOMACY: STUDIES IN THE DETERMINANTS OF FOREIGN POLICY. New York: Praeger, for the School of Advanced International Studies, Johns Hopkins University, 1966. 210 p. Paperback.

A provocative collection of essays synthesizing various influences on the foreign policy of African independent states, worthy of further study and replication.

73   Nkrumah, Kwame. CHALLENGE OF THE CONGO: A CASE STUDY OF FOREIGN PRESSURES IN AN INDEPENDENT STATE. New York: International Publishers, 1970. 295 p.

A detailed, and often turgid, interpretation of partial truths, attributing the ills of the former Belgian Congo mostly to external intervention by imperialist powers. It was presumably written after Nkrumah's fall from power.

74   Shepherd, George W., Jr. NONALIGNED BLACK AFRICA. Lexington, Mass.: Heath, 1970. 143 p.

A review of the international behavior of African states under the confusing notion of nonalignment, with the help of the systems approach. Substantive issues, organized in chapters, include inter-African rivalries; the 1964 Stanleyville paratroop drop; Rhodesia; liberation movements; and relations with Europe, Communist states, and the United States. African states are seen as nonaligned to the extent that they consciously pursue decision-making autonomy and interact systemically. Small powers are seen as either aligned or nonaligned. African states derive growing international influence from a global trend toward pluralism, and their greatest contribution may be to sensitize the world to greater moral responsibility.

75   Skurnik, W.A.E. THE FOREIGN POLICY OF SENEGAL. Evanston, III.: Northwestern University Press, 1972. 297 p. Tables, charts, bibliography.

The foreign relations of a moderate African state, reviewed from the points of view of pre- and post-independence continuities, internal and external institutional devices, cultural and economic components, and nonalignment. The author applies some of the concepts of Rosenau's "pre-theory" and suggests their adaptations for the study of nonwestern foreign policy.

76   Thiam, Doudou. THE FOREIGN POLICY OF AFRICAN STATES. New York: Praeger, 1965. 127 p.

A thoughtful essay by a former foreign minister of the Republic of Senegal. It distinguishes between ideological foundations of African foreign policies (nationalism and socialism) and realities (keeping and strengthening independence, as well as various conflicts), and discusses political and economic aspects of ties with extra-African powers.

77   Thompson, W. Scott. GHANA'S FOREIGN POLICY, 1957-1966. Princeton, N.J.: Princeton University Press, 1969. 437 p. Appendices.

A presentation of Nkrumah's foreign policy as a series of missed opportunities. The author had access to people and papers after Nkrumah's ouster by his armed forces. Although much less radical than his popular image, Nkrumah nonetheless suffered from a "lack of any sense of proportion," which distorted his self-importance and his image of his country and which produced a sad lack of realism.

78   Vandenbosch, Amry. SOUTH AFRICA AND THE WORLD: THE FOR-
      EIGN POLICY OF APARTHEID. Lexington: University of Kentucky
      Press, 1970. 287 p. Bibliographical note.

      A historical account beginning with the seventeenth century
      when the area became important in world affairs. The approach
      is balanced rather than venomously opposed to apartheid, al-
      though the author suggests that the government must adapt do-
      mestic change to external pressure.

Chapter 2

WESTERN EUROPE AND AFRICA

A. SUBSTANTIVE INTRODUCTION

The 1960s will long be remembered as the modern decade of Africa's independence. By 1974 only the Spanish Sahara in west Africa and the French Territory of the Afar and Issa [Djibouti] in the east remained under European colonial control. The Portuguese territories (Guinea-Bissau, Mozambique, and Angola) were achieving independence. But the legacy of Europe in Africa is everywhere. New African elites adopted languages, food, value preferences, ideologies, and scientific methods. New political systems intended to be national and democratic used largely European models. More than a decade after most African states became independent, Western Europe remains the predominant foreign influence in Africa. The survival of European commercial, intellectual, cultural, social, and to a much lesser degree security ties is the most significant feature of Africa's relations with the rest of the world. Europe is still Africa's major trading partner and its source of external assistance; less tangible bonds have proved resilient and withstood the criticism of purists. The resulting relations with Western Europe are complex, somewhat contradictory, and fluid. They include rejection of European tutelage, the need for aid, a desire for emulation, and the resentment of past and present injustices. (The available international relations literature concentrates on France, Britain, and Portugal, with little available on Belgium, Spain, and other European countries.)

European colonialism began haphazardly, involving mostly the search for trade, activities of some religious missionaries, and a few experiments with European settlement. The thoughtless scramble which followed the Franco-Prussian War and led to control of Africa in two decades was inspired by European interests, intended to substitute expansion and conquest in Africa for expansion and conquest in Europe. Once hegemony had been achieved, Europe rapidly lost interest in its new possessions. The Second World War was a watershed in European-African relations. Allied nations first needed manpower and raw materials to fight for their survival and, subsequently, African markets to recover from the disaster. By then colonial powers were generally so weakened that they also lost most of their determination to continue their domination, particularly in the face of growing African nationalism and the high cost of alternatives.

Sizeable public aid programs, however slowly and hesitantly implemented, launched the colonies on the road to modernization. Most important, the prewar strings of Africans educated in European and American universities came to fruition; Africans turned concepts like self-determination on their mentors, whom they shrewdly accused of hypocrisy for not practicing in Africa what they preached at home.

In the fifteen years between the end of World War II and political independence for the new African states, French governments set out to accomplish impossible political objectives in Africa. Despite French resistance to increasing African demands for autonomy and independence, this period was one of slow devolution of political control from France to Africa. Much of the literature on this subject concentrates on the reluctance of French leaders to envisage independence for Africa and emphasizes obstacles to independence inherent in the French political system. The most significant obstacles can be summarized briefly. The first was the notion of the indivisibility of the French Empire or Republic and the consequent conceptual difficulties French leaders had in breaking the unitary mold governing relations with colonial areas. The second was the swift erosion of the French's gratitude for the Africans' enormous aid in defeating Germany and the resulting reassertion of special-interest colonial groups and of ossified French government bureaucracies to preside over their overseas wards. The third was the general immobilism of the French political system, which contributed to conservatism in colonial policy. The last was the fear that France would lose its worldwide role, which encouraged continued devotion to a French unitary system encompassing 100 million Frenchmen. Only in this way, it was believed, could France hope to compete successfully with the superpowers and preserve its past grandeur.

However, most former French territories became independent in 1960, whereas most of the former British colonies were not granted independence until later years. Thus, despite powerful centralizing preferences, French decolonization policy was never behind that of other colonial powers. The major reasons were that political relations between the metropole and the territories had long developed in the direction of separation and that French policy, never as consistent as Cartesian principles might suggest, was very adaptable to new realities.

Franco-African political relations at first moved in a unitary mold. Africans had representatives in the French legislature, served in various organs of the French executive, and participated in numerous advisory bodies. But two developments worked against centralization. One was, ironically, the Africans' close association with metropolitan politics. At first Africans welcomed the opportunity to participate in making decisions at the center, but they soon found that the decentralized nature of French politics created divisions among them and that a choice had to be made between their African and French interests. African politicians, while continuing their association in France, also began to express demands for basic changes in this relationship.

32

Western Europe and Africa

The second development which undermined continued centralization was the implantation after World War II of autonomous political structures in the African territories. Created to serve as the basis for central representation in France, these structures resulted in unanticipated eventual separation through territorial legislatures and African political parties which aggregated and maintained popular support. This created a fundamental constitutional and political conflict about legislative and later executive autonomy in Africa. When African structures gained strength and separate legitimacy, this could not be reconciled with French constitutional requirements for subordination, for a French parliament could not both delegate and retain sovereignty. Continued French sovereignty would have required a firmness on the part of French governments which was not forthcoming. African leaders at first accepted federalism in their relations with France because they saw no viable alternative, but their acceptance weakened in time with the growing influence of African interests and eventually yielded to demands for a divisible entity that recognized their right to independence.

The transformation of the two colonial federations (West and Equatorial Africa) had special significance in this context. They were created to serve French rather than primarily African interests, were temporary structures, and were officially discarded by Paris when they had outlived their usefulness. The postwar decision to permit embryonic political life in Africa was anchored in the territories rather than at the federal level, because political boundaries were already established, and because of increasing French awareness of the ethnic differentiation, immense distances, and economic diversity between the separate territories. When the French legislature mandated the executive to implement reforms in 1956 which created nearly autonomous territories, the decentralization trend was strengthened. The French faced two levels of authority, federal and territorial, as well as African demands for more territorial autonomy. It chose to increase the authority of the territories, thereby weakening inter-African federal structures. The Africans resolved the conflict between territorial and federal levels of authority by opting for the territorial. The federal, inter-African system worked well while imposed from above, but it was abandoned once the French fiat was removed and was replaced by incipient territorial, political, and economic nationalism. Examination of these events challenges the currently accepted belief that the Europeans, in this case the French, were responsible for balkanizing Africa; the Africans could have maintained the federations but elected not to do so after French support was withdrawn.

The final stage of Africa's accession to political independence came after the collapse of the French Fourth Republic. French leaders at that time overestimated their ability to continue French suzerainty over the restive African territories and worked with excessively legalistic formulas. But French behavior after 1958, insensitive as it was to African demands, accelerated independence. General de Gaulle's early opposition to official recognition of the Africans' right to independence yielded a policy of temporary containment, but it deeply offended Africans and reinforced their determination to seek full political sovereignty. Consequently, they achieved the full political independence they had been requesting.

33

Although the French empire disappeared, French influence in Africa is still significant. It enjoys important economic influence. Also, its relations with the new states are generally friendly, and its prestige is high. Among the many reasons for continued close relations, three are particularly strong: economic ties, favorable predispositions of attitudes, and strategic considerations.

Most of the former French African territories are among the poorest in the world, and they have received little aid from richer countries. African leaders are very much aware, in theory, of the desirability of diversifying their external economic relations, particularly since independence. They know, however, that only France has maintained a deep and abiding interest in them. Franco-African economic relations were structured in a "hunting" preserve closed to outsiders; these structures have persisted since independence, although they are becoming less important to France and more undesirable to the Africans. Most of the African's commercial exchanges take place with the former metropole, and prices are arbitrarily high. The currency used in former French Africa (with few exceptions) is backed by the French franc, and the system encourages fiscal conservatism. French bilateral economic assistance remains vital. French contributions increased after independence, and French governments have prided themselves on the fact that their aid to developing countries, most of which has gone to Africa, is the greatest national effort of any donor country. From a post-independence vantage point, the integrationist objectives of French economic policy now appear to constrain the African states in unforseen ways. The program was too ambitious, and the maintenance of impressive buildings, highways, and bureaucracies deflects revenue from development. This situation compels France to continue aid so that economic collapse in Africa does not mar France's prestige. In fact, prestige is one of France's chief motivations for continuing aid. The traditional French desire to shine abroad, and fears that France might no longer be a power with world interests, account for much of the commitment. Foreign aid is "the only means to assure for France . . . a real place in the world, to avoid a degradation of French prestige" ("Dossier sur la politique francaise d'aide au tiers-monde." Paris: Ministere de la cooperation, 1966. 2 p. Mimeographed). The leaders of former French Africa understand this and have used it to their advantage.

The economic relations between France and Africa have drawn criticism and praise. A balance sheet is inconclusive, however, because the elements are not easily comparable. From a strictly short-range economic viewpoint, the advantage lies with the recipients. The French have often nudged their African friends to become more self-reliant. From a political and psychological viewpoint, the answer is less clear and depends upon intangible criteria. Demands for complete independence, younger African cadres, diversification of economic ties, changing notions of self-sufficiency, and French reluctance to continue aid are all combining to open the system.

France's defense interests in Africa are an outgrowth of colonial doctrine, and they stand out for their formal and legal aspects. In this area French thinking about Africa was less flexible than on political concerns, and French policy did not change until the mid-1960s when France withdrew most troops, leaving behind only a few units to defend presumably common interests. After the Portuguese, French troops are the most potent foreign military force in Africa, although they represent only a vestigial French interest. Franco-African defense agreements contain elements of continuity and change. Military aid for African national armed forces, which had to be created from scratch (Africans were integrated in larger, colonial units), includes material, training, and instruction. The major problem of French assistance is political—endemic instability, the speed and relative simplicity of African military coups d'etat, and the political repercussions of intervention. Paris has thus become prudent and has lowered its profile. The wisest course for France now is to remove its military presence, since the intense nationalism in Africa now is not compatible with foreign military presence.

Finally, because of long association, there is a favorable disposition toward Africa among the French public. The French have taken an assimilationist stance toward colonial populations and have desired to see French culture emulated. This concept, derived from ideals of the French Revolution, assumes that the various peoples with whom the French came into contact were fundamentally equal. Since they had not yet reached the height of European (French) civilization, France was obligated to make these benefits available to them. Thus, they sought to turn Vietnamese or Senegalese into yellow or black Frenchmen. Once provided with a French education and sensitized to French culture, earlier differences would vanish and the assimilation process would be completed, according to this philosophy.

In practice, of course, this was never achieved on a large scale. Nonetheless, thousands of Africans are proud of their association with French civilization, and even younger Africans who reject their French heritage on intellectual grounds adhere to many French norms at the behavioral level. As nationalism has increased since the 1930s, African intellectuals have proclaimed that they, not the French, must decide which standards to assimilate and which to reject. This sensitive dilemma has not yet been settled.

Franco-African relations are changing; the partners are growing apart. The Africans are becoming increasingly restive about cooperation agreements signed as a quid pro quo for their political independence, and French leaders show some misgivings for continuing a concentrated relationship which, in the long-run, may not be worth the price.

On the relations of Britain to her former colonial territories very little has been written in this country. Accounts of the colonial past are abundant, and there is some literature about British ties with southern Africa. The reasons for the lack of material on contemporary issues are not clear. American scholars view the independence of Britain's former African territories as somehow more complete than that of other states and, hence, perhaps conclude that not much need be said about the subject. Also, cultural and linguistic familiarity with the British may engender approval of the British separation in Africa among American scholars and skepticism about the experiences of Latin countries. The ties between Britain and Africa remain significant, and they deserve more attention. Americans are much better informed about domestic developments in the former British states than the French ones and have sometimes idealized former British states for their presumed similarity to the United States. It does seem, however, that the overall pattern of international relations, specifically of the end of the colonial period, is best viewed as a closely comparable phenomenon.

British-African relations have evolved through a pattern similar to Franco-African ties. Independence came in the 1960s, and Britain, like France, granted political independence for a variety of motives. These included the growth of nationalism and of modern political structures and attitudes in Africa, Britain's receding international role as a result of World War II, its domestic economic weakness, and its unwillingness to pay the price for continued control by military means.

British post-independence relations with its former African dependencies are also comparable to those of France. Political, economic, and security ties continued at first but have since been diluted. Aid programs were implemented before independence and were considerably expanded afterward. British contributions to such assistance were less spectacular than their French counterparts but were nonetheless substantial. As in the case of France, British aid was highly concentrated in former possessions. Decisions about and size of aid flows were determined by a number of factors, including a general commitment to aid developing areas and Africa in particular, internal demands giving priority to domestic needs, feelings of closeness toward former British areas, considerations of prestige, and fiscal conservatism. Economic relations remained structured in the British pattern after independence, and the Africans still depended on Britain, if only for lack of viable alternatives. British firms which have strong preferences for continuing existing commercial ties tend to dominate the modern sector of the economy.

The most signal changes in Britain's ties with Africa have occurred in security and military policies. Two major factors account for this. First, the African states inherited quasi-national military structures which could simply be transferred to the new governments. By the end of the 1960s there was no British military presence or direct influence in Africa, and the separation required assistance only in material, training, and technical personnel. The agreements between Britain and Africa were less formal than their French counterparts. Nonetheless, London showed no inclination to continue direct military involvement, and such involvement is unlikely in the future unless it has the active support of Britain's allies.

The second major reason for discontinuing security relations dates back to the granting of independence for India in 1947. India was always the major focus of the British empire, with Africa of secondary importance, a mere station enroute to the Orient. Once Britain relinquished control over India, its attachment to Africa declined further. Historically, Africa had been of greater strategic importance to France than to Britain. British colonial manpower during World War II, for instance, was drawn mostly from Asia; the French

depended chiefly on Africa. The importance of Africa declined even further
when Britain decided in the late 1960s to withdraw security interests east of
the Suez Canal.

There are two notable exceptions to this pattern of rapid withdrawal and devolution of responsibility. Both involve the issue of neocolonialism and, consequently, raise powerful emotions. One concerns the Republic of South Africa and Britain's willingness to sell weapons to that country's white minority
government at a time when white South Africans gird themselves to confront
possible insurgency, from either domestic or foreign origins. Nonetheless, in
view of Britain's strong economic ties with South Africa, its willingness to
abide by an international arms embargo against South Africa was an indication
that British governments are not insensitive to the decolonization issue. (South
Africa continued to purchase arms from European countries until it was self-
sufficient; weapons sales to South Africa by the French were hardly made an
issue by Africans, to the dismay of some observers.)

The other exception, Britain's policy toward southern Rhodesia, generated criticism which overshadowed the favorable aspects of the British decolonization
process. In this case, the British were criticized not for selling arms, but
for not using their own military muscle in behalf of an African cause. Since
Rhodesia was a British dominion at the time its government declared the country independent (1965), the British government, as well as African independent
states and most western powers, considered this problem a British responsibility.
For a number of reasons British governments preferred negotiations and pressures
applied through the United Nations to direct intervention in what was techni-
cally a rebellion against the Crown. African and other critics were incensed
at what they considered Britain's failure to take the necessary remedial action.
Clearly no British government will easily intervene at a time of retrenchment
from overseas commitments and severe domestic economic problems. This conflict involved differing estimates of British responsibilities in Africa, and the
situation in Rhodesia probably will not be strongly affected by public discussion.

Another similarity between French and British relations with Africa is Africa's
declining importance to the former metropoles. European commercial relations
with Africa have not grown nearly so rapidly as with other parts of the world.
Britain's decision to join Europe after having been a global, imperial power
for many centuries should affect its foreign trade and investment. The British
no longer believe their continued influence in Africa will result in adoption
of British-style parliamentary democracy, efficient government, bureaucratic
structures, as well as pride in the colonial legacy. Africans are instead finding their own ways.

Nevertheless, many differences exist in the policies of France and Britain in
Africa. Whether these are seen as basic or merely matters of degree and
style may depend upon estimates of the importance of human relations. But
the former French and British states differ in their economic viability, in educational policy, in the resilience of traditional structures, in predispositions

toward eventual independence, and in concepts of foreign policy. Any student of Africa can easily puncture these generalizations; they are intended as a general overview rather than as a detailed account.

First, the former British states are wealthier than their French counterparts. Britain placed greater emphasis on economic criteria. The very poorest among the African states tend to be French, landlocked, and arid. Second, the British provided some modern education to a larger percentage of Africans, and they stressed technical training, whereas France aimed at the highest possible academic achievement. Third, Britain ruled its colonies indirectly, using traditional African structures as ancillary arms to its bureaucracy, and thus these structures have remained strong. The French ruled directly, replacing native structures with imported bureaucrats and thus weakening the African structures. The effect of this distinction remains, however, a subject for debate. Fourth, Britain seemed to envision an eventual separation, which the French seemingly did not. Or perhaps the British simply accepted the inevitable and were not concerned about justifications.

Finally, the British have long valued flexibility in their foreign relations. Unlike the French, they escaped humiliation through occupation in World War II, and presumably they had no need for salving such wounds at the expense of colonial possessions. In this sense, Britain acted like a queen of pragmatism.

American observers at times express admiration of Britain for having done the proper thing at the proper time and in the proper manner. One eminent student has suggested that "the British exit from Africa . . . has been one of the most reasonable and amicable end-processes in the recorded history of imperialism" (Nielsen, GREAT POWERS, p. 73). It is not certain, however, that an economically prosperous and politically strong Britain would have been as reasonable and amicable. Seldom are questions raised about possible relationships between economic hardship at home and readiness to let colonies that were economic burdens go their own way. Systematic, comparative inquiry into such matters would be beneficial.

Another sphere in which Britain differed from France was in human relations. The French had a reputation for a more humane position on race relations than did the British. Africans in both former French and British territories were understandably marked by European cultural values. They may call each other "saxophones" and "francophonies," but the European imprint is likely to resist overnight extirpation, and some prominent African leaders believe it will remain.

When one considers results, the differences between France and Britain were not nearly so important as the similarities. The French, British, and Portuguese have experienced the same swift breakdown of their careful assumptions about the direction and timetable of African independence. Among the recent Western European colonial powers, Portugal stands out for obstinate refusal to accept the era of decolonization and its determination to hold on to its African empire by force. A combination of factors underlies this refusal,

including poverty and domestic authoritarianism which contributed to insensitivity toward African demands for economic growth and political liberalization,
a long and proud history of colonialism refractory to a new era, a sense of
destiny expressed in multiracial ideals within Portugal's political philosophy,
a fear of contamination through liberalization elsewhere, a sense of injustice
at the international furor which Portugal's colonial policy attracted and, more
recently, hopes for some economic rewards.

Portugal's authoritarian political system was for a long time untouched by the
democratic revolutions in the rest of Europe. Effective political power was
centralized and was supported by conservative military, commercial, religious,
and landed elites. Portugal, a poor, backward country not yet caught up
with modern development, has been prevented by the weight of the past from
becoming "European."

Portugal's colonial expansion began at a time when such activity was estimable,
an admirable effort to evangelize and save souls otherwise consigned to eter-
nal damnation and to search for markets. The country became a world power
by the sixteenth century and seems never to have recovered from its fall from
that pinnacle. Africa did not become important to Portugal until the late
nineteenth century; the metropole was then neither a world power nor fully
European and had difficulty in maintaining its own identity in isolation. Portugal held on to economically unprofitable colonies because of pride, the
structure of social and class interests, the relative ease of continued domination, delusions about noble myths, and a sense of historically or divinely
inspired imperial destiny. The new dream was that of a unified whole anchored in Portuguese nationalism: "Lusitropicoply," summarized as the creation of a "new type of civilization . . . by transforming the tropics, not by
introducing European values but by themselves changing into Lusitropicals in
body and soul." This new state was to be achieved "through miscegenation
and . . . through socially Christianizing non-Europeans rather than through
culturally europeanizing them" (Chilcote, PORTUGUESE, p. 48).

Contemporary observers judge Portugal harshly and believe its policy must
change; future judgment may be more mellow. Portugal's response to worldwide opprobrium stressed the purity of Portuguese motives over pragmatic adjustment to change. Couched in logical terms, the defense emphasized the
moral relativity of current United Nations debates, the false expectations of
political independence, and the fallacies of such absolutes as self-determination and one-man, one-vote. Portuguese spokesmen reminded Africans that
their new political systems are far different from their leaders' professed ideals
and suggested that the gap between ideal and performance is a human failing
rather than a fault of Portuguese colonialism.

Portugal nevertheless could not remain immune from the development of African nationalism and could not prevent others from claiming the same right.
In April 1974 the Portuguese military accomplished what other domestic elites
had long resisted: they seized power in Lisbon, proclaimed the end of the
domestic political system, and indicated their readiness to grant independence

to the African territories through political negotiations rather than through
continued armed conflict.

Most of Western Europe entertains diplomatic and economic ties with Africa.
Switzerland, for instance, operates an effective though little known aid program. Aside from France, Britain, and then Portugal, the most significant are
Belgium and the Federal Republic of Germany. Belgian involvement in Zaire
(the former Congo, whose capital city was renamed Kinshasa from Leopoldville)
has attracted global attention since its brusque independence in 1960. The
issues which developed were complex and intensely emotional. They helped
create a profound inter-African split. The use of mercenaries to fight insurgents created bitterness. The conflicts caused the death of Patrice Lumumba,
widely admired as a symbol of African nationalism, and of a United Nations
secretary-general. They also initiated a rift between African states and Russia
about the role of the United Nations, and they attracted charges of Russian
cold war games and American imperialist designs. It was only in the late
1960s that Zaire restored normal relations with the former colonial power.
Belgian presence and influence in Zaire remains considerable, as in the other
former Belgian territories of Rwanda and Burundi, and Belgium has contributed
substantially to economic development.

The West Germans' new pragmatism in Africa, and their economic strength, are
overcoming memories of past colonial brutalities. Once the restrictive Hall-
stein doctrine was abandoned, the Federal Republic entered into economic
agreements with nearly all African states. The Germans' attitude has gained
many Africans' respect and confidence, although Germany's influence will be
limited so long as it avoids political involvement. Germany contributes as
much as does France to the multilateral development fund of the Common
Market, far in excess of expectations.

One of the most significant aspects of relations between Western Europe and
nearly half the African states is these states' association with the European
Economic Community (EEC). The association, which antedates independence,
was created in 1957 at the insistence of France, partly to shift to Europe some
of the burdens of economic assistance. The association is designed to enhance
trade between the EEC and the eighteen associated African members and to
contribute to African growth through the European Development Fund (EDF), a
multilateral channel for grants beyond bilateral aid programs. The EDF pro-
visions were renegotiated after independence to cover the years from 1963 to
1969 and subsequently to run to January 1975. Future agreements are likely
to diversify African-European relations, but must be seen also in the context
of global economic developments. This experiment in international relations
has attracted considerable attention and a number of advocates and detractors.

Critics have suggested that an association between strong and weak nations
perpetuates neocolonialism, have expressed distrust of French intentions, have
claimed that the association is inimical to African unity, have argued that
western capitalist nations have sinister designs on Africa. They also have

charged that such agreements have a negative effect on pan-Africanism and have deplored preferential relations as inhibiting the growth of global trade and Africa's ability to compete freely in world markets. Advocates have pointed out that association has opened up markets for additional African exports through agricultural and other diversification. They have said it is no bar to inter-African economic cooperation and is a departure from exclusive ties with a colonial country and thus the kind of multilateralization the African wants. They also have noted the lack of any immediate practical alternative.

American observers have disagreed widely on the proper role of Europe in Africa, often in relation to their views about American policy in general in that area. Some, who hoped to end the decolonization process swiftly, attribute its continuation to recalcitrant European influence. With that influence removed, the United States could play its rightful role to help liberate Africa from oppression. Others fear a chaotic period in Africa and thus prefer continued European involvement with a marginal American role. Some believe that a strong Europe is needed as a building bloc for world security and should not be weakened by detaching Africa from it. Finally, some have chided Europeans as a collection of selfish, opportunistic powers pursuing separate national interests instead of adopting a common all-African policy. They believe that the United States will not meet its responsibilities in Africa, and they assume that a united Western European policy would.

The future role of Europe in Africa is likely to be more limited, one based on greater attention to specific issues and on loosening colonial and post-colonial ties. Changing European assessments facilitate disappointments--real and perceived--about the importance of Africa. And Africans are beginning to take a second look at prospects for complete independence and the end of exploitation. Change will not be abrupt, and some dependence, regarded as cooperation, will continue. But both Africa and Europe are beginning to diversify their economic and other relations, entailing lower costs and more widespread opportunities.

B. ECONOMIC RELATIONS

79   Dumont, Rene. FALSE START IN AFRICA. Translated by Phyllis Nauts Ott. New York: Praeger, 1966. 303 p. Appendices, charts, paperback.

A searing but sympathetic indictment, widely resented by African governments, calling for fundamental change in development strategies, mostly in former French Africa. The author is an agronomist. The writing is well informed and fast paced, and the message is optimistic.

80   Mazrui, Ali A. "African Attitudes to the European Common Market." JOURNAL OF INTERNATIONAL AFFAIRS (London) 38 (January 1967): 24-35.

An examination of the bases for rejection of formal ties with the Common Market. Opposition came chiefly from African leaders' suspicions and their desire for equality. It fell into three categories: first, objection to European Unity on the grounds that it could lead to European independence and concomitant downgrading of Africa; second, objection to direct ties lest these continue European dominance; and third, acceptance of some economic ties, but without formal political links that imply obligations leading to unwanted African dependence.

81   Okigbo, Pius N.C.   AFRICA AND THE COMMON MARKET.   Evanston, Ill.: Northwestern University Press, 1967. 169 p. Tables.

A report by Nigeria's representative in negotiations, begun in 1963, about association with the European Common Market. The book reports on these talks and describes the development of the Common Market and its other African associates. Okigbo then discusses prospects for an African common market, examining theoretical and practical considerations. African-European cooperation requires consideration of political versus economic benefits and a greater emphasis on political criteria, particularly in view of the declining European interest in African trade compared with trade with other nations.

82   Rivkin, Arnold.   AFRICA AND THE EUROPEAN COMMON MARKET: A PERSPECTIVE.   Rev. ed. Denver: Social Science Council/Graduate School of International Studies, Monograph no. 4, 1966. 58 p. Tables, appendices, paperback.

A brief but cogent review of the association of eighteen African and six European states, its evolution, and its future prospects. The association is viewed as mutually beneficial because there are no acceptable alternatives.

83   Zartman, I. William.   THE POLITICS OF TRADE NEGOTIATIONS BETWEEN AFRICA AND THE EUROPEAN COMMUNITY: THE WEAK CONFRONT THE STRONG.   Princeton, N.J.: Princeton University Press, 1971. 228 p. Tables.

An examination of the negotiations leading to renewal of the original agreement, the first detailed account available in English. The emphasis is on how the poor negotiate with the rich. The negotiations are analyzed as a political bargaining process which yields important insights and shows that in this case (given the European commitment), the poor are not necessarily powerless.

C. FRANCE

84   Adloff, Richard. WEST AFRICA: THE FRENCH-SPEAKING NATIONS
YESTERDAY AND TODAY. New York: Holt, Rinehart and Winston,
1964. 315 p. Mpas, appendices, paperback.

A primer on the history, people, economy, and politics of the
former colonial federation by a long-time, sympathetic student.
The last chapter sketches developing relations with the world
and in inter-African affairs.

85   Corbett, Edward M. THE FRENCH PRESENCE IN BLACK AFRICA.
Washington, D.C.: Black Orpheus, 1972. 197 p. Tables.

Chiefly a discussion of the elements of French influence--social,
political, economic, and military--remaining in black Africa.
The book is detailed and schematic, but contains nothing new.
It expresses a distaste for what is termed French cultural imperialism.

86   Foltz, William J. FROM FRENCH WEST AFRICA TO THE MALI FEDERA-
TION. New Haven, Conn.: Yale University Press, 1965. 196 p. Appendices, bibliography, tables.

A skillful, classic analytical study of the breakup of the Mali
Federation in 1960, of its antecedents, and of implications for
political unification among African independent states. The
treatment is generally favorable to the cause of the Soudan,
and it is complemented by a content analysis of the two former
partners' major newspapers.

87   Hargreaves, John D. WEST AFRICA: THE FORMER FRENCH STATES.
Englewood Cliffs, N.J.: Prentice-Hall, 1967. 168 p. Maps.

A brief introductory history of French expansion, with some
attention to the events leading to independence.

88   Hayter, Teresa. FRENCH AID. London: Overseas Development Institute, 1966. 216 p. Tables, paperback.

A solid, well researched study of France's foreign aid programs,
before and after African independence, by a rare anglophone
who understands the French. Such aid to Africa has been
"massive" and, though not free from the burdens of the colonial era, is adapted to African needs, at times after considerable French prodding.

89   Lewis, William H., ed. FRENCH-SPEAKING AFRICA: THE SEARCH
FOR IDENTITY. New York: Walker, 1965. 236 p. Paperback.

43

One of the first introductions into former French Africa published in this country. It is a collection treating political,
social and cultural, and economic problems and their evolution with a section on foreign policy.

90   Lusignan, Guy de. FRENCH-SPEAKING AFRICA SINCE INDEPENDENCE.
      New York: Praeger, 1969. 381 p. Maps, bibliography.

      A well documented, historical narrative of political and some
      economic developments since Charles de Gaulle. The book is
      divided into three parts: one on the coming of independence,
      one on post-independence events and trends, and one assessing
      international situations. The conclusion is that some progress
      was made, but not so much as hoped for or as is possible.

91   Morgenthau, Ruth Schachter. POLITICAL PARTIES IN FRENCH-SPEAKING
      WEST AFRICA. Oxford: Clarendon, 1964. 434 p. Appendices,
      pp. 378-434.

      A detailed historical survey of the evolution of political rela-
      tions which culminated in independence, with special attention
      to Senegal, the Ivory Coast, Guinea, and the former Soudan,
      as well as a chapter on the Mali Federation.

92   Mortimer, Edward. FRANCE AND THE AFRICANS, 1944-1960: A
      POLITICAL HISTORY. New York: Walker, 1969. 371 p. Maps.

      A thorough but often confusing account of developments from
      1944 to national independence in 1960. It is useful primarily
      for specialists as background material.

93   Neres, Philip. FRENCH-SPEAKING WEST AFRICA FROM COLONIAL
      STATUS TO INDEPENDENCE. London: Oxford University Press, for
      the Institute of Race Relations, 1962. 101 p. Maps, paperback.

      A compact review of the historical background and of accession
      to independence, focusing on colonialism and its erosion and
      examining the structural arrangements of the Franco-African
      community.

94   Senghor, Leopold Sedar. ON AFRICAN SOCIALISM. Translated by
      Mercer Cook. New York: Praeger, 1964. 165 p.

      A collection of essays by Senegal's foremost political leader
      which reveal his early concepts of nationalism and African
      socialism.

95   Toure, Sekou. EXPERIENCE GUINEENNE ET UNITE AFRICAINE. Paris:
      Presence Africaine, 1961. 559 p. Paperback.

A detailed record of the deterioration of Guinea's relations
with France from 1958.

96 _____. LA POLITIQUE INTERNATIONALE DU PARTI DEMOCRA-
TIQUE DE GUINEE. Conakry: Imprimerie 'Patrice Lumumba, 1961.
276 p. Paperback.

A collection of speeches by the "enfant terrible" of French
Africa and president of Guinea in the three years after his
country's independence. The topics are international and inter-
African affairs.

D. GREAT BRITAIN

97 Alexander, H.T. AFRICAN TIGHTROPE: MY TWO YEARS AS NKRU-
MAH'S CHIEF OF STAFF. New York: Praeger, 1966. 128 p. Illustrations, appendices.

Some personal insights into the structure and evolution of Ghana's armed forces, of United Nations service in the Congo,
and of the complex nature of Nkrumah's personality in the
three years from 1959 to 1961.

98 Austin, Dennis. BRITAIN AND SOUTH AFRICA. London: Oxford
University Press, for the Royal Institute of International Affairs, 1966.
177 p. Tables, appendices.

A lucid analysis of British interests in South Africa and the
former High Commission Territories, including a detailed discussion of economic and strategic factors. The author reviews the
pros and cons of international sanctions against the apartheid
regime and reluctantly concludes that they would create more
problems than they would solve.

99 Good, Robert C. UDI: THE INTERNATIONAL POLITICS OF THE
RHODESIAN REBELLION. Princeton, N.J.: Princeton University Press,
1973. 327 p. Illustrations.

A thorough historical review of the events and pressures which
led to and followed the declaration of independence in 1965.
As a student of Africa, former State Department official, and
ambassador to Zambia, the author combines understanding, sympathy, and knowledge. He suggests that Britain could have
intervened in 1965 only with extraordinary difficulty and that,
since violent change is Inevitable, the international system
(chiefly the western powers) has an obligation to contribute
to the solution of Rhodesia's internal problem and consequently
should shun halfway measures like sanctions.

100 Kirkwood, Kenneth. BRITAIN AND AFRICA. Baltimore: Johns Hopkins

Press, 1965. 235 p. Index.

A broad examination of British-African relationships. The first three chapters trace the evolution of British involvement in Africa from before the First World War until about 1964. Chapters 4 through 6 concentrate on relations with southern, eastern, and western Africa. A concluding chapter is far reaching and examines such topics as the advantages for Africa of continued, post-independence association and cooperation with Britain; the characteristic British, pragmatic dislike for defining objectives with any precision, leading to misunderstanding and dissatisfaction by more insistent partners; the hope for an enlarged commonwealth; approval of the gradualist process leading to African independence; the need for sharing responsibilities in Africa with other nations; and the "particular merits of Africo-British qualities" as a constructive infusion into the new states.

101   Newbury, Colin W. THE WEST AFRICAN COMMONWEALTH. Durham, N.C.: Duke University Press, for the Duke University Commonwealth Studies Center; London: Cambridge University Press, 1964. 97 p.

A review of select facets of the evolution of and justifications for British rule and of modern and traditional African elites. The book also discusses relations between Britain and her former west African colonies and concludes that the isolated, noncontiguous states tend to draw away from the Commonwealth, although they expect that Britain's behavior be "exemplary," a legacy of British expectations transferred to Africa.

E. PORTUGAL

102   Abshire, David M., and Samuels, Michael A., eds. PORTUGUESE AFRICA: A HANDBOOK. New York: Praeger, in cooperation with the Center for Strategic and International Studies, Georgetown University, 1969. 465 p. Maps.

A selection of essays on the historical, political, economic, and international relations issues and developments of Portuguese colonialism. They provide background against which to evaluate contemporary events, and the book's interdisciplinary nature is particularly welcome.

103   Chilcote, Ronald H. PORTUGUESE AFRICA. Englewood Cliffs, N.J.: Prentice-Hall, 1967. 128 p. Bibliographic note, maps, paperback.

A discussion of the history of the Portuguese overseas empire and of Portuguese and African nationalism, followed by a review of developments in the African territories. The roots of colonialism are seen in Portugal's social, political, and economic structures; hence, its fate will be decided in Lisbon rather than Luanda or Lourenco Marques.

104   Duffy, James. PORTUGAL IN AFRICA. Baltimore: Penguin, 1963.
       229 p. Maps, paperback.

       A review of Portugal's involvement in Africa, emphasizing the
       passage from Portuguese hopes to disappointment, the distinc-
       tions between reality and theory, and the growing internal and
       external difficulties to which Portugal must eventually yield.

105   Henricksen, Thomas. "Portugal in Africa: A Non-Economic Interpreta-
       tion." AFRICAN STUDIES REVIEW 16 (December 1973): 405-16.

       A timely corrective to a prevailing emphasis on Portugal's eco-
       nomic motives for colonialism in Africa. This brief study sug-
       gests that noneconomic factors may be as potent as, if not more
       potent than, economic ones in explaining Portugal's failure to
       adjust to changing times.

106   Minter, William. PORTUGUESE AFRICA AND THE WEST. Baltimore:
       Penguin, 1972. 179 p. Appendices, paperback.

       A discussion contending that Portugal's colonialism in Africa is
       "ultracolonialism," simultaneously the most extreme and primi-
       tive form of that general phenomenon. Portugal remains in
       Africa because it is primitive and, therefore, inflexible. Lib-
       eration movements in the former Portuguese territories are seen
       as fighting the battle against global imperialism. One chapter
       discusses the armed struggle in Africa, another the policy of
       the United States, and another the help given Portugal by
       Europe and Brazil.

107   Nogueira, Alberto Franco. THE THIRD WORLD. London: Johnson
       Publications, 1967. 154 p. Paperback.

       An analysis, written by a former Portuguese foreign minister,
       which affords clear insight into the motivations of that country
       to hold on so long in Africa. They are, essentially, a refusal
       to bow to developments regarded as logically inconsistent and
       inappropriate from the vantage point of universal principles of
       morality, although pragmatic adjustment would have counseled
       a different policy.

108   Wheeler, Douglas L., and Pelissier, Rene. ANGOLA. New York:
       Praeger, 1971. 253 p. Appendices, select bibliography, maps, illustra-
       tions, index.

       A competent review divided into separate but complementary
       parts. Part 1 presents historical materials on the country and
       its long relations with Portugal, and part 2 focuses on domestic
       unrest, with special reference to African liberation movements

and the Portuguese response until about 1970. A brief essay
discusses Angola's place in southern Africa and future prospects.

Chapter 3
THE UNITED STATES AND AFRICA

A. SUBSTANTIVE INTRODUCTION

American policy toward Africa developed rapidly, at the first signs of the new states' independence in the late 1950s. It reflected relative ignorance about Africa and only occasional, distant interest. The question of a desirable American policy will no doubt be debated for many years to come. Present trends seem to point toward decreasing attention to Africa, with some exceptions.

Official American policy toward Africa may be approached in different ways, each providing some understanding. Before such distinctions are made, it should be remembered that Africa seemed remote to Americans until the end of World War II. Except for historical connections with Liberia dating back to the nineteenth century, and the Italian attack on Ethiopia in the 1930s, there was little concern for Africa. Similarly, for the period after 1945 when Western Europe still controlled most of Africa, the United States made few attempts to deal with Africa as a separate entity. Official American concern, therefore, came only with impending or actual independence and dates from the late 1950s.

Three approaches predominate in the literature. One is chronological. It differentiates an era of ignorance, lasting until either 1950 or 1958, from an era of selective attention since then. Another approach distinguishes periods of successive presidents and administrations since 1945. A third approach concentrates on particular issues or problems singled out as case studies; examples include examinations of policy toward Nigeria, Zaire, or southern Africa.

Attempts to single out determinants of American policy since African independence turn up numerous relevant factors. Specific interests or events may be discrete or fit a more general pattern of variables, depending upon the focus used. The following themes can be extracted from public information about American policy, their relative potency varying with circumstance: (1) the search for a new, American global role; (2) a tradition of sympathy for the underdog, in this case for colonized peoples; (3) slow elaboration of new

American government structures which must compete for attention and resources with older bureaucracies; (4) desire for free access to markets and raw materials, viewed with trepidation by Europeans; (5) strategic concerns derived chiefly from extra-African interests; (6) stirrings of responsiveness to novel and diffuse domestic special interest groups; (7) assistance for African aspirations; (8) a low overall priority assigned to things African; (9) avoidance of significant and/or direct involvement in African problems; and (10) prevention of great power rivalry, lest it be detrimental to the United States.

Perhaps the single most important factor in American policy toward Africa is a strong reluctance to become directly involved. This reluctance is a major thread running through policy, although it is not always explicit. It has created resentment among those who suggest that the United States has moral or other obligations to intervene on behalf of African interests. All American policy toward Africa, except for responses to need for humanitarian assistance, reveals this nonintervention theme. It can be illustrated by the first crisis in America's Africa policy, the 1960 request by the new Congolese government for military assistance to help maintain internal security and later national integrity. This topic still engenders lively debate, usually on some ideological ground.

The American response was based on fears of Soviet inroads on American ideals of freedom and self-determination and on some economic motives, though less so than antiwestern analysts suggest. What is often overlooked or forgotten is that the American government chose not to send marines or mercenaries but to call on the United Nations, a telling indicator that the Congo was not vital to American interests. Since Khrushchev at that time saw developing countries as a choice arena for Soviet intervention, it is not surprising that American policy makers responded in part in cold war terms. Washington hoped to defuse the dangers of Russian intervention by interposing the United Nations, and that success would discourage further attempts. In this instance, an African country was not worth direct American government intervention. This policy guideline has not changed substantially.

The cold war, on examination, was a much less potent factor in determining American policy than it seems on the surface. As a motivating factor, it was incidental rather than commanding. Two aspects of American cold war mentality were visible in the late 1950s and early 1960s. One was related to perceptions of African ability to withstand the kind of Communist influence that could be detrimental to American interests. Peaceful nonviolent evolutionary change in Africa was regarded as strengthening an international environment compatible with American values and processes. It was also considered capable of resisting Communist encroachments. This meant American encouragement for majority rule, government by consent of the governed, and respect for national minorities as the type of political structure most likely to prevent Communist inroads. It meant also that Algerian-type uprisings should be avoided because they provided innocent but perhaps dangerous openings for Communist interference. The second aspect of cold war mentality related to Western Europe.

Given the predominance of Western Europe in global American thinking, and the American belief that an economically sound Europe was the most effective bulwark against communism, the United States encouraged the new African states to continue their relations with Europe; in this sense, the interest of Africa was seen as subsidiary to those of Europe.

A complementary approach could concentrate on the dynamics of the evolution of American policy in Africa and be sensitive to features of the changing global, African, and American environment as policy determinants. American policy in 1976 is clearly not what it was in 1959. Such an approach could distinguish further between two periods: one of discovery, encompassing the late 1950s and early 1960s, and one of reaction and distraction which followed. It is tempting to suggest that the United States has regarded Africa as important in its own right only in the flush of novelty and idealism which followed the new states' independence. The three or four years surrounding 1960 were marked by respectable increases in economic aid, the appointment of top officials sympathetic to Africa, the influx of younger and better trained foreign service officers to the new Africa Bureau, unprecedented symbolic votes of the United Nations, and a certain excitement about things African generally.

Great expectations derived not only from the Kennedy aura and the promise of support for Africa "because it is right"; they reflected also an image of the United States whose glitter had not yet withstood the test of time. The African image of the United States included a heritage of anti-colonialism and the Atlantic charter; early opposition to a French return to Indochina; independence for the Philippines; sensitivity to the legitimacy of nonalignment for developing countries; and commitment to a vast program of economic assistance which could be easily tapped by newcomers to the world scene. Such euphoric views were soon replaced by disappointment and frustration, as state relations were established and images gave way to interests. In 1966 it was still possible to mobilize widespread humanitarian and political support for the cause of Biafra. But by the end of the decade and in the early 1970s, Americans had other concerns, and Africa seemed once more remote.

The second period of American policy toward Africa, one of cooler calculation as much as distraction by other events, actually began in the early 1960s. The Bay of Pigs debacle, renewed tensions in Berlin, and the Cuban missile crisis shifted U.S. administration concerns away from Africa toward competition with Russia and toward a greater reluctance to offend European countries. New concerns occupied American officials, including the consequences of misadventure in Southeast Asia and its implications for the role of the United States in the world and growing domestic American problems.

Since then U.S. policy toward Africa has been characterized by a withdrawal of initial rhetoric and hopes; a new emphasis on low cost, low risks, and a low profile; and an underlying assumption that African issues were less significant than other major problems. Two brief examples will illustrate the policy shift. Both concerned southern Africa: the November 1965 decision of the Rhodesian government to declare that country independent from Britain and the

attempt to wrest control of South West Africa from the Republic of South
Africa. In both cases, the United States was careful not to be involved directly or to assume major risks. On the Rhodesian issue, Washington followed
Britain's lead and approved mandatory sanctions by the United Nations; this
was done to demonstrate commitment to the principle of majority rule and to
be counted on the side of justice. On the South West Africa issue, the United
States actively supported UN declarations to the effect that South Africa
had forfeited its mandate over that territory, again a commitment to principles
commanding nearly unanimous global approval. But actual American commitments in both cases were minimal. Neither the votes nor the declarations at
the United Nations, nor the forgoing insignificant trade and investment rewards,
were of any great consequence for the United States.

By 1975, American policy in Africa had fallen victim to a new realism which
reflected concern with global rather than African issues and which focused
greater attention on domestic problems. Africa's claims on American attention
and resources had to compete with relations with Russia and China, as well as
with energy shortages and inflation. The new realism came about also as a
result of doubts about an earlier faith in American help toward nation-building,
apparent lack of interest by top political leaders and administration officials,
and an assessment that significant involvement would yield insignificant rewards.
The earlier simplistic American image of Africa as a novel and noble human
experiment was tarnished by events and impressions mediated by the press and
accumulated over time. America's new image of Africa, in many ways equally
simplistic, included chronic instability, fratricidal massacres, intemperate public
statements, and diplomatic voltes-faces. Americans also showed growing resentment of constant rhetoric assailing American imperialism, of criticism of American aid as insufficient handouts, and of simultaneous suggestions that the United
States was somehow responsible for solving African problems not if its making.

American economic relations with Africa consist of foreign assistance and trade
and investments. Offical aid includes mostly that provided by the Agency
for International Development (AID), the Peace Corps, and loans and grants
under Public Law 480, which was originally intended to dispose of agricultural
surpluses. American aid to Africa has several special features. First, and
perhaps most important, it is viewed as supplementary to aid from other donors,
chiefly the former colonial powers. Although the United States contributes
about 20 percent of all bilateral aid flowing into Africa, it spends less than
most donor countries on economic assistance, currently about two-tenths of
1 percent of its gross national product for the entire developing world. Second, American aid suffers from a number of handicaps related to earlier high
expectations. The Marshall Plan mediated the false impression that economic
growth anywhere abroad needed only a brief infusion of capital and technical
aid; only in the 1950s was it understood that conditions in the Third World
require long-range aid to achieve visible results. The intensely ideological
cold war period made justifications for prolonged aid to developing states
relatively easy, and it also nurtured expectations of gratitude and political
support on the part of recipient states. In 1959, a U.S. Senate study concluded that "it is clear that . . . aiding African states to achieve economic

ends . . . will pay rich returns in friendship and respect for the United States" (Senate, U.S. FOREIGN POLICY, p. 315). More recently questions have arisen about the desirability of aid to offset the Communist threat. It is perhaps ironic that the importance of the cold war to the United States declined shortly after African independence and the brief Kennedy-Khrushchev interlude. Whatever the meaning of peaceful coexistence or detente, the concepts have inaugurated a downgrading of aid to Africa by the United States.

Third, foreign aid does not benefit from the kind of national support which many other federal activities enjoy. Fourth, the present public mood is one of retrenchment from overseas involvements, and all aid is increasingly difficult to justify to the public and its elected representatives.

Other factors are important in understanding public American aid to Africa. The criteria which help determine aid recipients include (1) actual and potential markets for American goods; (2) actual or potential political influence of recipient states; (3) political rewards by friendly governments; (4) concentration of bilateral aid on eight "development emphasis" states—Liberia, Ghana, Nigeria, Zaire, Ethiopia, Kenya, Tanzania, and Uganda; (5) increasing emphasis on regional, multidonor, and small individual self-help programs; (6) support for private investment; and (7) special attention to southern African independent states to help them overcome heavy dependence on white-ruled areas.

During the period from 1948 to 1967 the African continent received 2.9 percent of all American economic aid. Between 1969 and 1974, sub-Saharan Africa's share came to $1.1 billion. Appropriations for Africa rose sharply for a few years after independence and then declined: from $80 million in 1958 to a peak of $325 million in 1972, down to $235 million in 1973. Africa has ranked at or near the bottom of the geographic areas, depending on the aid category inspected.

American aid is given also to civilian security forces under a "Public Safety" program. Precise statistics are not available, but most of this assistance is provided abroad; some personnel are trained at the International Police Academy located in Washington, D.C. Finally, Africa's share of Peace Corps volunteers is much larger than its share of overall assistance: between 25 percent and 30 percent of all volunteers have served in Africa. In 1971, there were 2,700 volunteers in Africa, the largest contingents in Sierra Leone, Ghana, and Liberia. They tend to be highly concentrated with nearly 80 percent in twelve African states. The American economic assistance program in Africa was summed up by former Assistant Secretary of State David Newsom in the following terms: "It was my hope that . . . I could help to sustain and increase America's efforts in the development of Africa. That hope has not been fully realized" ("African Development and U.S. Foreign Policy," November 2, 1973, p. 3. Typescript).

American trade with Africa has grown significantly in absolute terms since about 1960, but it remains a small percentage of total U.S. foreign trade.

53

To the United States, trade with Africa is still marginal in terms of value and quantity; it amounts to slightly more than trade with Australia and Oceania. American exports to Africa were about 3.9 percent of total exports in 1960 and 1970, and imports from Africa decreased from 3.7 percent in 1960 to 2.8 percent of global imports by 1970. Obstacles to trade growth include American lack of familiarity with Africa, the Europeans' tendency to view former colonies as their "reserves," African economic nationalism, the dearth of foreign trade structures, shortages of foreign exchange, small and fragmented markets, and low per capita income. Nevertheless, American trade is now more diversified and prospects for growth are good. American dependence on Africa for raw materials will likely expand, since Africa has a considerable share of world resources for such materials as manganese, copper, antimony, chromium ore, gold, petroleum, bauxite, and diamonds.

American direct private investment in Africa followed the same pattern as trade: it grew substantially, but represents only a small fraction (below 4 percent in 1970) of total U.S. investments abroad. Its value was about $300 million in 1950, and it reached $4 billion by 1970. The share of South Africa declined from more than one-half to less than one-third of the total for the continent, and that of independent black Africa rose from next to nothing to one third; this distribution probably will shift even more toward independent states.

It has been customary to distinguish clearly between the U.S.'s national and special economic interests in Africa. Aid is usually regarded as national, whereas trade and investment are private. This distinction likely will be refined in the future, and some special interests may relate closely to the national interest. The need for raw materials, for instance oil from Nigeria, is of concern to more than the businessmen involved. Government policy may transform private connections into a national issue, such as the importation of chrome ore from Rhodesia or the policies of businesses toward economic and social conditions of their employees. Another such issue is the extent and desirability of unchecked private corporate power and its effects on the well being of African peoples. This theme is discussed frequently under the label of imperialism which, according to critics, should be corrected by appropriate government action.

America has no vital security interests in Africa. The United States has neither an alliance treaty with Africa nor combat troops stationed in Africa. Facilities on land in an era of strong nationalism are no longer in vogue, and they are being turned over to the host country. The few strategic interests are related to matters external to Africa. The most significant remaining U.S. strategic interests include overflight and landing rights, sophisticated electronic monitoring devices, and a space tracking station operated in the Republic of South Africa. In the last few years American policy makers concerned about access to petroleum and Soviet naval activities have shown new strategic interests in littoral states of the Indian and South Atlantic Oceans. But the price the United States is willing to pay for such considerations is not yet clear. Some data illustrate the absence of significant American interest.

American military assistance to the continent, between 1950 and 1972, was the lowest for any geographic region receiving such aid. It ranged between $15 million and $30 million per year, equivalent to about 1 percent of all American military aid. Most of this aid has gone to sub-Saharan Africa ($12.1 million worth of the total of $15.9 million, for instance, in fiscal year 1972). In black Africa the aid is highly concentrated, and with two exceptions (Ethiopia and Liberia), it is intended as a supplement. Ethiopia received most of the U.S. military aid during this period, more than 90 percent of that given to sub-Saharan Africa. The remainder has gone mostly to five other states, Nigeria, Zaire, Liberia, Mali, and Ghana. (For further details, consult MILITARY ASSISTANCE AND FOREIGN MILITARY SALES FACTS [May 1973]. Washington, D.C.: Department of Defense, Security Assistance Agency [1973].)

Since the mid-1960s, the American government has decreased grants of military aid in favor of sales for either cash or credit. Given the poverty of Africa, that area could not be expected to contribute more than a small fraction of total sales. In 1972, for example, sub-Saharan Africa purchased only one-third of 1 percent of global American sales of military equipment; Zaire accounted for 85 percent of the purchases, with the rest being bought by Liberia and Nigeria. The Defense Department also offers training for foreign military personnel, both in the United States and abroad. In the twenty-two years since 1950, about 8,000 personnel from the African continent (some 2 percent of the world total) received such training, of whom 60 percent (4,980) were from black Africa. Ethiopia was highly favored, with 60 percent of the black African total; other states included, in order of descending importance, Zaire, Liberia, Ghana, the Sudan (each more than 100), as well as Mali, Upper Volta, Senegal, and Guinea.

American military assistance must also be understood against the backdrop of that region's total expenditures and external assistance. African states obtain most of their security aid from the European former metropolitan countries and from a few independent suppliers, which together account for more than two-thirds of the total. For the continent, the average annual increase in defense outlays decreased from 9.6 percent for the period between 1949 and 1969 to 5 percent in 1969. In that year the continent spent $1.2 billion on defense, and thirteen black African states spent $820 million. In fiscal year 1969 the United States provided less than 3 percent of these countries' defense expenditures in military assistance.

Although the security value of Africa is inconsequential for the American government, such ties nevertheless have significant political meanings. These may be more important than the strict security issues, but they nevertheless raise questions of costs affecting African-American relations and the consequences of developments for America's overall interests. Two examples illustrate this problem. One concerned American involvement in Ethiopia, the political implications of which came to public light after a congressional investigation in 1970. The issue became a dilemma after the ouster of the Ethiopian emperor in 1974. Public disclosures about American involvement were not new, but this incident merely escalated the mounting criticism of American foreign policy in general. Ethiopia's armed forces, chiefly with American support, were built up to more than 40,000 men as tacit payment for the Kagnew communications facility in Eritrea, a rebellious province since its integration into Ethiopia in 1962, but also a strategically located one. Much criticism focused on the possible implications of a 1960 agreement affirming America's "opposition to any activities threatening the territorial integrity of Ethiopia" (Senate, HEARINGS: U.S. SECURITY AGREEMENTS, p. 1905). This was interpreted as opening the door to U.S. interference in Ethiopia's affairs, particularly in view of domestic coups d'etat, of American weapons used to contain Eritreans, and of Ethiopian hostilities with a neighboring state.

Another American action related to security which caused considerable political repercussions was a series of American-Portuguese agreements reached in 1970, designed to insure continued American access to Lajes air base on the Azores island of Terceira. The agreements made available to Portugal, as a NATO member, unprecedented amounts of direct and indirect economic assistance totaling about $450 million. These agreements were extraordinary. First, the amount of the aid was nearly twice the annual American aid to Africa. Second, the justifications were both strategic and economic. According to Washington, the Azores were needed for anti-submarine surveillance and as a staging and refueling area for planes. Educational reforms in Portugal were to be financed by the U.S. Defense Department, perhaps a novel venture for that establishment. Economic benefits were to accrue from a $400 million Export/Import bank loan to promote American exports.

The agreements no doubt made a good deal of sense, but taken in context with Portugal's anachronistic colonial wars in Africa, their negative political implications were bound to overshadow any such merit. To Africans they suggested incomparable insouciance and insensitivity to African commitments to self-determination. Accordingly, they were widely interpreted as a callous gesture of American support for an immoral Portuguese cause. The agreements were thus seen as hypocritical, and they damaged U.S. relations with Africa for years to come.

No aspect of American policy has generated as much discussion and controversy as that which concerned southern Africa. Some observers have suggested that because the area's problems differ fundamentally from those elsewhere in Africa, the American response ought to reflect the difference, whereas American policy has accepted the distinction only in rhetoric and not in fact. U.S. policy can be summarized briefly. Conditions are not such that they invite a clearcut solution; rather, they involve painful, partial choices which satisfy no one fully. U.S. policy has combined practical and moral considerations, and it has embodied the idea that the United States should be responsive to the region but without claiming to have full responsibility. It has attempted to conciliate divergent pressures and interests and has been influenced by five major concerns.

The first involves symbolic public declarations of support for self-determination and majority rule and a concurrent rejection of violence. Second, the U.S. has applied diplomatic pressures to encourage negotiations among the parties involved. Third, the U.S. has avoided moves that may jeopardize American interests in the rest of Africa or create frictions with or among NATO members. Fourth, in assessing the short-term external and internal forces in southern Africa, the U.S. has concluded that basic change must be generated from inside, that "the key fact of southern Africa is the power of the whites and the will to use it to maintain white domination" (Hance, SOUTHERN AFRICA, p. 8). Finally, the United States has a determination to avoid direct involvement in another foreign area.

The United States has taken some concrete steps to implement policy. In regard to South Africa, these include an international arms embargo involving some financial losses quickly taken advantage of by others, chiefly European nations; encouragement of American business firms to improve working conditions for their employees to the full extent permitted by law; support for pressures to deprive South Africa of its League of Nations mandate over South West Africa (Namibia); and special assistance to the former High Commission Territories to help offset their economic dependence on the Republic. In relation to Rhodesia, the American government has refused to recognize the legitimacy of that country's independence. It has also faithfully supported mandatory United Nations sanctions until the Congress partially voided executive action, and given special assistance to Zambia, which was hardest hit by these sanctions. Finally, regarding Angola and Mozambique, the U.S. government repeatedly opposed Lisbon's military activities and secured an agreement that Portugal not use in Africa weapons supplied for NATO purposes. Although the United States was one of a very few countries which honored these commitments throughout the 1960s, implementation of some was relaxed in the 1970s.

Available policy options were discussed during the debate on how to bring about fundamental change in southern Africa through international sanctions against incumbent regimes. A variety of such measures, from disengagement to total boycott, were considered, and each raised issues transcending regional perspectives toward Africa or southern Africa. The distinction made between Rhodesia, against which total sanctions were adopted, and South Africa, against which they were considered and rejected, reveals the practical limits of policy measures by the United States and other nations. The difference resulted not so much from ideology as from the costs involved.

By African standards South Africa is an economic giant; its economy is moving toward self-sufficiency, is the most modernized, and generally considered healthy. The U.S. decided that sanctions against South Africa, though desirable in some ways, would be impractical. Complex logistic, economic, financial, and attitudinal difficulties made it doubtful that the countries which would have to bear the costs—chiefly Western Europe and the United States—would do so. Past experiences with international sanctions against a powerful state were not encouraging. Moreover, since the Republic was capable of resisting sanctions for an indeterminate period, prospects for harming the disfranchised majorities were greater than for ending the discriminatory system of apartheid. The debate on sanctions was followed by another on the alternative of disengagement. The term is imprecise but covers several general types of options: verbal condemnations; symbolic disengagement, including the curtailment of economic and diplomatic contact; an "economic negative" tactic consisting of moves against future trade and investment; and an "economic positive" tactic, meaning business initiatives to raise workers' standard of living. Although the term "disengagement" has not been used to describe official American policy, the United States has used the first and last of these options.

In Rhodesia the United States has supported a total boycott and has regarded continued rule by white minorities as a threat to international peace. American interests in that country are negligible, and thus are the material costs of sanctions. In this case, therefore, it was relatively easy to combine principle and prudence. The issue nevertheless touched off a major public controversy in this country because of the foreign policy principles involved. The debate, between idealists and realists, involved the basics of international policy. Idealists argued that the United States had a moral obligation transcending the system, an imperative which a great nation cannot evade. Violations of human rights anywhere can be a threat to peaceful intercourse among nations, since they involve emotional issues which cut across national borders. Moreover, since Rhodesia is not independent, international action is not illegitimate intervention in its domestic affairs.

Realists have suggested that there are no absolutes in international morality or in political representation and participation. Since moral postures are transient, the world must rely on procedures for an acceptable modicum of permanence and predictability. Finally, realists have contended that a policy based on expediency clothed as morality is a hypocritical gesture, and that singling out one country for violating human rights because that country is weak is an instrumental policy, not a moral one.[1] From the American government's point of view, sanctions against Rhodesia were intended less to bring about an immediate transfer of political power than to sustain the legitimacy of eventual decolonization in southern Africa. In this sense, subsequent action by the U.S. Congress to eviscerate sanctions seemed obtuse and insensitive.

The most serious criticism of American policy in southern Africa is drawn from a broader historical perspective and involves the end of an era and birth of a new one. It regards decolonization and self-determination as inherent human rights, and it requires the transfer of power from minority to majority, particularly when minority rule is based on skin color and symbolizes racial oppression.

---

1. These arguments are symbolized in an exchange of letters between former Secretary of State Dean Acheson and Supreme Court Justice Arthur Goldberg in the WASHINGTON POST. The issues are discussed more fully in Nielsen, GREAT POWERS, pp. 317-20.

Some American and foreign critics have endowed the United Nations and western powers with special responsibilities on the decolonization issue, and they were bound to be bitterly disappointed. They have tended to view American, and by extension western, policy as timid and palliative. They have criticized the West's collective reluctance to use its enormous means, implying it has been involved in a silent conspiracy to maintain the status quo. These judgments seem harsh and perhaps unrealistic, but the feelings aroused in oppressed people of the world are powerful and cannot be ignored.

The arguments that the national interests of the United States cannot be defined so narrowly as to exclude support for decolonization in southern Africa is often countered by the specter of another Vietnam, presumably involving American military action to rescue American citizens trapped in an African revolution. But another Vietnam in southern Africa is not so certain, and the threat may simply be intended to arouse fears and influence minds.

For those with a deep commitment to human rights it is difficult to justify American policy in southern Africa. The desires for just treatment of the nonwhite majorities are in line with traditional American values and current efforts to live up to them. Racial discrimination in the United States is regarded as disreputable and hence cannot be condoned elsewhere. Commitment to such values exerts a strong pull on one's conscience and creates a painful dilemma if one also evaluates seriously the hard realities of American involvement. Refugees from Eastern Europe, for instance, can testify to the debilitating effect of false hopes for American intervention on their behalf. But policy makers have an obligation to consider what is possible in addition to what is desirable and to be aware of the limits of American influence.

B. GENERAL LITERATURE

109 Attwood, William. THE REDS AND THE BLACKS. New York: Harper & Row, 1967. 334 p. Illustrations.

A highly engaging memoir by a journalist and former ambassador to Guinea and Kenya during the Kennedy and early Johnson years. Among the issues recounted are negotiations surrounding the 1964 paratroop drop in Stanleyville. The writer benefited from a noncareer envoy's personal relationships in Washington and freedom from conventional diplomatic style. But his account also emerges as more enthusiastic than profound. He denigrates "cold warriors" while suggesting means for outfoxing the Russians.

110 Bowman, Larry W. SOUTH AFRICA'S OUTWARD STRATEGY: A FOREIGN POLICY DILEMMA FOR THE UNITED STATES. Athens: Ohio University Center for International Studies, Africa Series no. 13, 1971. 25 p. Paperback.

An argument urging that America really choose sides and support the forces of change before it is drawn into the South African conflict regardless of intentions.

111 Chester, Edward W. CLASH OF TITANS: AFRICA AND U.S. FOREIGN POLICY. New York: Orbis Books, 1974. 279 p. Tables, indexes.

A description of select aspects of relations between the United States and Africa. Only the last three chapters are devoted to the period after the Second World War. The book has the merit of looking at the entire continent, but it suffers from lack of clarity and any organization other than chronology. Hence, the specialist or even the interested generalist will gain little from it.

112 Emerson, Rupert. AFRICA AND THE UNITED STATES. Englewood Cliffs, N.J.: Prentice-Hall, 1967. 110 p.

A primer on American policy until the mid-1960s written by a well known student of imperialism. The major point is that a period of disenchantment almost inevitably followed illusions and ignorance on both sides.

113 Goldschmidt, Walter, ed. THE UNITED STATES AND AFRICA. New York: Praeger, for the American Assembly, 1964. 295 p. Paperback.

A collection of essays on American interests and policy guidelines, as well as on African political, social, and economic problems. The themes represent a transition period of American understanding of a changing world. The brief chapter on U.S. government operations in Africa makes the book worthwhile.

114 Hance, William A., ed. SOUTHERN AFRICA AND THE UNITED STATES. New York: Columbia University Press, 1968. 167 p.

Four essays which review the policies of incumbent white elites and the political situation of the majorities in southern Africa, the implications for American policy, and the issue of American disengagement from South Africa. Based on the assumption that the white governments have the power and will to maintain themselves in office, the authors believe that the struggle for change will be protracted and that, given the relative importance of the area to the United States, American policy will involve few commitments and risks. The editor reviews the various moral, logical, prudential, economic, psychological, and political arguments for and against disengagement and suggests that the cost may be disproportionate to the results.

115 Hayford, Fred Kwesi. INSIDE AMERICA: A BLACK AFRICAN DIPLOMAT SPEAKS OUT. Washington, D.C.: Acropolis Books, 1972. 250 p.

A Ghanaian's rather superficial but passionate impressions of the United States; some of his observations and criticisms are astute.

116   Kennan, George F. "Hazardous Courses in Southern Africa." FOREIGN AFFAIRS 49 (January 1971): 218-36.

An eloquent argument that the countries of southern Africa should be allowed to solve their own problems without ill-conceived and moralistic external interference.

117   Lake, Anthony, and Park, Stephen. BUSINESS AS USUAL: TRANS-ACTIONS VIOLATING RHODESIAN SANCTIONS. New York: Carnegie Endowment for International Peace, Special Rhodesia Project, Interim Report, 1963. 60 p. Appendices, paperback.

A critical expose of some American firms which apparently violated the U.S. embargo on trade and financial relations with Rhodesia; the link with government policy is tenuous, although plausible.

118   Lefever, Ernest W. CRISIS IN THE CONGO: A U.N. FORCE IN ACTION. Washington, D.C.: Brookings Institution, 1965. 181 p. Appendices, paperback.

A balanced account of American efforts, through the United Nations, to prevent the first Congo crisis from becoming em-broiled in the cold war, with considerable attention to the structural and political problems involved.

119   _____. SPEAR AND SCEPTER: ARMY, POLICE, AND POLITICS IN TROPICAL AFRICA. Washington, D.C.: Brookings Institution, 1970. 221 p. Appendices.

A review of political problems in Africa and particularly in Ghana, Zaire, and Ethiopia which then turns attention to the African armed forces and police and American aid and policy toward the military. American influence in these matters is viewed as minor and usually constructive, at least in intent.

120   Marcum, John A. THE POLITICS OF INDIFFERENCE: PORTUGAL AND AFRICA, A CASE STUDY IN AMERICAN FOREIGN POLICY. Syracuse, N.Y.: Syracuse University Maxwell School of Citizenship and Public Affairs, Program of Eastern African Studies, no. 5, 1972. 41 p. Paperback.

A criticism of excessive American realism and support of private U.S. interests. Marcum calls on America to overcome its in-difference to help the cause of freedom.

121   Marshall, Charles Burton. CRISIS OVER RHODESIA: A SKEPTICAL

VIEW. Baltimore: Johns Hopkins University Press, 1967. 75 p. Paperback.

A review of the international uproar about Rhodesian independence to which the author brings to bear some history. He examines British insistence that majority rule be the price of independence, exposes the hollowness of abstract moral principle in international affairs, questions the legal and actual validity of the United Nations finding that Rhodesia represents a threat to peace, and suggests that procedures are more durable and practical in relations among states.

122　Melady, Thomas Patrick. BURUNDI: THE TRAGIC YEARS--AN EYE-WITNESS ACCOUNT. Maryknoll, N.Y.: Orbis Books, 1974. 94 p. Appendices.

A sensitive statement by a well known Catholic humanitarian, the American ambassador in a Burundi troubled by unrest involving more than 100,000 deaths. Unwilling to apportion blame, Melady reflects on the effects of alienation and fear and on the inability of the United States to influence either the country or the OAU to stop the racial killings.

123　Morris, Roger, et al. PASSING BY: THE UNITED STATES AND GENO-CIDE IN BURUNDI, 1972. Humanitarian Policy Studies Special Report. New York: Carnegie Endowment for International Peace, 1973. 49 p. Paperback.

An assessment of difficult policy choices relating to massacres in Burundi. They are reviewed on the basis of value commitments and, predictably, are found wanting.

124　Morrow, John H. FIRST AMBASSADOR TO GUINEA. New Brunswick, N.J.: Rutgers University Press, 1968. 284 p.

An interesting memoir by an American professor of romance languages whom Eisenhower sent to Guinea. The author is deeply sympathetic to the cause of African independence. He lacks the thick skin of a professional diplomat, a factor related somewhat to his return to his chosen calling.

125　Nielsen, Waldemar A. AFRICAN BATTLELINE: AMERICAN POLICY CHOICES IN SOUTHERN AFRICA. New York: Harper & Row, for the Council on Foreign Relations, 1965. 184 p.

An analysis, written by a former president of the African-American Institute, which details American policy alternatives in the Portuguese territories, Rhodesia, South Africa, the High Commission Territories, and South West Africa. He calls for greater dynamism in policy to encourage change in the area, in cooperation with other powers.

126　Pomeroy, William J. APARTHEID AXIS: THE UNITED STATES AND
SOUTH AFRICA. New York: International Publishers, 1971. 79 p.
Appendices, paperback.

A sharp critique of American policy seen as at least partially
responsible for the continuation of apartheid in South Africa.
The United States is seen as abandoning its moral role.

127　Rivkin, Arnold. AFRICA AND THE WEST: ELEMENTS OF FREE WORLD
POLICY. New York: Praeger, 1962. 212 p. Charts, paperback.

A review of African development problems with emphasis on
the European Economic Community, Israel, and the United Nations. Rivkin sees American policy as applying general principles toward Third World countries to the newer African states
and as inherently flexible. The emphasis is on stability, peaceful evolution, and cooperation with Europe. The writer assumes that African democratic, rather than authoritarian,
states are a prerequisite for economic growth and are most
compatible with American interests.

128　Smith, Stuart [pseud.]. U.S. NEOCOLONIALISM IN AFRICA. New
York: International Publishers, 1974. 253 p. Index, paperback.

A treatment of economic, social, ideological, and military
aspects of American imperialism by a research fellow at the
Russian Institute of World Economy and International Relations.
It is the only book-length, straight Marxist analysis of the
subject available in English.

129　Weissman, Stephen R. AMERICAN FOREIGN POLICY IN THE CONGO
1960-1964. Ithaca, N.Y.: Cornell University Press, 1974. 303 p.
Bibliography.

A Marxist assessment in which the author suggests a strong ("not
one-to-one" causal) relation between the class background of
American decision-making elites and U.S. policy. American
concerns in the early 1960s about African leaders' ability to
resist Communist pressures can be explained in a number of
ways, and thus it seems reasonable that several of these, and
not just one, could be valid.

130　Williams, G. Mennen. AFRICA AND THE AFRICANS. Grand Rapids,
Mich.: Wm. B. Eerdmans, 1969. 218 p.

A useful book for the uninitiated, written by a former assistant
secretary of state for African affairs (1961-66). The first two
parts treat general topics, with some attention to competition
with Communist countries and to southern Africa. Part 3 is on
American policy. The book is fast-paced, frequently anecdotal,
and shows the well intentioned enthusiasm of the era of the
New Frontier.

C. CONGRESSIONAL DOCUMENTS

131   House. Committee on Foreign Affairs. THE FACES OF AFRICA: DI-
VERSITY AND PROGRESS; REPRESSION AND STRUGGLE--REPORT OF
SPECIAL STUDY MISSION TO AFRICA. 92d Cong., 2d sess. 21 Sep-
tember 1972. 471 p. Appendices.

132   _____. REPORT OF SPECIAL FACTFINDING MISSION TO NIGERIA.
91st Cong., 1st sess. 12 March 1969. 59 p. Appendices.

133   _____. REPORT OF THE SPECIAL STUDY MISSION TO AFRICA.
89th Cong., 2d sess. 1 June 1966. 97 p. Appendices.

134   _____. REPORT OF THE SPECIAL STUDY MISSION TO SOUTHERN
AFRICA. 91st Cong., 1st sess. 6 November 1969. 179 p. Appendices.

135   _____. REPORT ON UNITED NATIONS USE OF PEACEKEEPING
FORCES IN THE MIDDLE EAST, THE CONGO, AND CYPRUS. 89th
Cong., 2d sess. 25 February 1966. 14 p. Appendix.

136   House. Committee on Foreign Affairs, Subcommittee on Africa. HEAR-
ING: AFRICA AND THE CHALLENGE OF DEVELOPMENT. 90th Cong.,
2d sess. 25 July 1967, and 24 April, 8 and 14 May 1968. 114 p.
Tables, appendices.

137   _____. HEARING: AFRICAN BRIEFING--1968. 90th Cong., 2d sess.
23 July 1968. 18 p.

138   _____. HEARING: THE CRISIS OF THE AFRICAN DROUGHT. 93d
Cong., 2d sess. 19 November 1974. 46 p. Appendices.

139   _____. HEARING: THE DROUGHT CRISIS IN THE SAHEL. 93d Cong.,
1st sess. 16 July 1973. 224 p. Appendices.

140   _____. HEARING: FOREIGN POLICY IMPLICATIONS OF RACIAL
EXCLUSION IN GRANTING VISAS. 91st Cong., 2d sess. 4 February
1960. 49 p. Appendix.

141   _____. HEARING: IMMEDIATE AND FUTURE PROBLEMS IN THE
CONGO. 88th Cong., 1st sess. 14 March 1963. 22 p.

142   _____. HEARING: MINORITY RULE AND REFUGEES IN AFRICA
(THE ROLE OF THE ALL-AFRICA CONFERENCE ON CHURCHES). 93d
Cong., 1st sess. 23 July 1973. 82 p. Appendices.

143 _____. HEARING: POLICY TOWARD AFRICA IN THE SEVENTIES. 91st Cong., 2d sess. 17, 18, 19, 23, 24 March; 19, 20, 21 May; 4 June; 30 September; 1 October; 18 November; and 3 December 1970. 361 p. Tables, appendix.

144 _____. HEARING: THE POSTWAR NIGERIAN SITUATION. 91st Cong., 2d sess. 27 January 1970. 21 p.

145 _____. HEARING: REPORT OF THE SPECIAL COORDINATOR FOR NIGERIAN RELIEF. 91st Cong., 1st sess. 24 April 1969. 23 p.

146 _____. HEARING: REPORT ON PORTUGUESE GUINEA AND THE LIBERATION MOVEMENT. 91st Cong., 2d sess. 26 February 1970. 25 p. Appendix.

147 _____. HEARING: REVIEW OF STATE DEPARTMENT TRIP THROUGH SOUTHERN AND CENTRAL AFRICA. 93d Cong., 2d sess. 12 December 1974. 38 p. Appendix.

148 _____. HEARING: SOUTH AFRICA AND UNITED STATES FOREIGN POLICY. 91st Cong., 1st sess. 2, 15 April 1969. 83 p. Appendices.

149 _____. HEARING: UNITED STATES INFORMATION AGENCY OPERA-TIONS IN AFRICA. 87th Cong., 2d sess. 7 February 1962. 22 p.

150 _____. HEARINGS: BRIEFING ON AFRICA. 86th Cong., 1st sess. 5 March and 21 July 1959. 20 p.

151 _____. HEARINGS: BRIEFING ON AFRICA. 86th Cong., 2d sess. 20, 26, 27 January, and 16 May 1960. 142 p.

152 _____. HEARINGS: CRITICAL DEVELOPMENTS IN NAMIBIA. 93d Cong., 2d sess. 21 February and 4 April 1974. 80 p. Appendix.

153 _____. HEARINGS: IMPLEMENTATION OF THE UNITED STATES ARMS EMBARGO (AGAINST PORTUGAL AND SOUTH AFRICA, AND RELATED ISSUES). 93d Cong., 1st sess. 20, 22 March, 6 April 1973. 398 p. Appendices.

154 _____. HEARINGS: IMPLICATIONS FOR UNITED STATES LEGAL OBLIGATIONS OF THE PRESENCE OF THE RHODESIAN INFORMATION OFFICE IN THE UNITED STATES. 93d Cong., 1st sess. 15, 17 May 1973. 176 p. Appendices.

155 _____. HEARINGS: UNITED STATES BUSINESS INVOLVEMENT IN

SOUTHERN AFRICA. 92d Cong., 1st sess. Part 1: 4, 5, 11, 12 May; 2, 3, 15, 16, 30 June; and 15 July 1971; Part 2: 27 September, 12 November, 6 and 7 December 1971; Part 3: 27, 28, 29 March, 3, 5, 6 April, and 13 July 1973. 620 p., appendices; 555 p., appendices; and 1,073 p., appendices, respectively.

156 _____. HEARINGS: UNITED STATES-SOUTH AFRICAN RELATIONS. 89th Cong., 2d sess. Part 1: 1, 2, 3, 8, 10, 15, 17 March 1966; Part 2: 23, 24, 30 March 1966; Part 4: 8 August 1966. 253 p., 136 p., and 30 p., respectively.

157 _____. REPORT AND HEARINGS: AFRICAN STUDENTS AND STUDY PROGRAMS IN THE UNITED STATES. 89th Cong., 1st sess. August 1965. 169 p. Tables.

158 _____. REPORT OF A SPECIAL STUDY MISSION TO AFRICA, CONDUCTED BY THE HONORABLE BARRATT O'HARA, ILLINOIS, CHAIRMAN OF THE SUBCOMMITTEE ON AFRICA. 91st Cong., 1st sess. 1969. 74 p. Appendices.

159 _____. REPORT OF SPECIAL STUDY MISSION TO WEST AND CENTRAL AFRICA. 91st Cong., 2d sess. 26 August 1970. 91 p. Appendices.

160 House. Committee on Foreign Affairs. Subcommittee on International Organizations and Movements. HEARING: UNITED NATIONS OPERATIONS IN THE CONGO. 87th Cong., 1st sess. 13 April 1961. 28 p.

161 _____. HEARINGS: ECONOMIC SANCTIONS AGAINST RHODESIA. 92d Cong., 1st sess. 17 and 22 June 1971. 123 p.

162 _____. HEARINGS: SANCTIONS AS AN INSTRUMENT OF THE UNITED NATIONS--RHODESIA AS A CASE STUDY. 92d Cong., 2d sess. 13, 15, and 19 June 1972.

163 House. Committee on Foreign Affairs. Subcommittee on the Near East and Africa. HEARING: ACTIVITIES OF PRIVATE U.S. ORGANIZATIONS IN AFRICA. 87th Cong., 1st sess. 8, 11, 12, 16, 25 May and 1 June 1961. 280 p. Appendices.

164 _____. HEARING: BRIEFING ON AFRICA. 86th Cong., 1st sess. 5 March and 25 July 1959. 20 p.

165 _____. HEARING: BRIEFING ON AFRICA. 86th Cong., 2d sess. 20, 26, 27 January and 16 May 1960. 142 p.

166   ____. REPORT OF THE SPECIAL STUDY MISSION TO AFRICA, SOUTH AND EAST OF THE SAHARA. 85th Cong., 1st sess. 5 April 1957. 151 p.

167   House. Committee on Foreign Affairs. Subcommittees on Africa and on International Organizations and Movements. HEARINGS: FUTURE DIRECTION OF UNITED STATES POLICY TOWARD SOUTHERN RHODESIA. 93d Cong., 1st sess. 21, 22 February, 15 March 1973. 200 p. Appendix.

168   ____. HEARINGS: THE REPEAL OF THE RHODESIAN CHROME AMENDMENT. 93d Cong., 1st sess. 15 and 17 October 1973. 152 p. Appendices.

169   ____. JOINT HEARING: UNITED NATIONS AND AFRICA. 92d Cong., 2d sess. 1 March 1972. 24 p.

170   House. Committee on Foreign Affairs. Subcommittees on National Security Policy and on Scientific Developments. HEARINGS: THE INDIAN OCEAN--POLITICAL AND STRATEGIC FUTURE. 92d Cong., 1st sess. 20, 22, 27, and 28 July 1971. 324 p. Appendix, index.

171   Senate. Committee on Appropriations. A REPORT ON UNITED STATES FOREIGN OPERATIONS IN AFRICA. 88th Cong., 1st sess. 23 March 1963. 803 p.

172   Senate. Committee on Foreign Relations. HEARING: UNITED NATIONS SANCTIONS AGAINST RHODESIA: CHROME. 92d Cong., 1st sess. 7 and 8 July 1971. 111 p. Appendix.

173   ____. HEARINGS: EXECUTIVE AGREEMENTS WITH PORTUGAL AND BAHREIN. 92d Cong., 2d sess. 1, 2, and 3 February 1972. 155 p. Appendix.

174   ____. HEARINGS: NOMINATION OF NATHANIEL DAVIS TO BE ASSISTANT SECRETARY OF STATE FOR AFRICAN AFFAIRS. 94th Cong., 1st sess. 19 February 1975. 80 p. Appendix.

175   ____. STUDY MISSION TO AFRICA, SEPTEMBER-OCTOBER 1961. 87th Cong., 1st sess. 14 January 1962. 17 p.

176   ____. UNITED STATES FOREIGN POLICY: AFRICA. (Prepared by the Program of African Studies, Northwestern University). 86th Cong., 1st sess. 23 October 1969. 84 p.

177   Senate. Committee on Foreign Relations. Subcommittee on African
       Affairs. HEARING: IMPORTATION OF RHODESIAN CHROME. 93d
       Cong., 1st sess. 6 September 1973. 111 p., Appendix.

178   Senate. Committee on Foreign Relations. Subcommittee on United
       States Security Agreements and Commitments Abroad. HEARINGS:
       UNITED STATES SECURITY AGREEMENTS AND COMMITMENTS ABROAD--
       ETHIOPIA. 91st Cong., 2d sess. (Part 8). 1 June 1970. 74 p. Index.

179   _____. Committee on Foreign Relations. And House. Committee on
       Foreign Affairs. HEARING: NIGERIAN-BIAFRAN RELIEF SITUATION.
       90th Cong., 2d sess. 4 October 1968. 89 p. Appendices.

180   _____. Committee on the Judiciary. Subcommittee to Investigate Prob-
       lems Connected with Refugees and Escapees. HEARING: AFRICAN
       REFUGEE PROBLEMS. 89th Cong., 1st sess. 21 January 1965. 62 p.
       Appendix.

181   Senate. Committees on Appropriations and on Commerce. STUDY MIS-
       SION TO CENTRAL AND EAST AFRICA, FEBRUARY 1971. 92d Cong.,
       1st sess. 21 June 1971. 19 p.

182   Senate. Committees on Foreign Relations, Appropriations, and Interior
       and Insular Affairs. STUDY MISSION TO AFRICA, NOVEMBER-DECEM-
       BER 1960. 87th Cong., 1st sess. 12 February 1961. 55 p. Appen-
       dices.

Chapter 4

THE SOCIALIST COUNTRIES AND AFRICA

A. SUBSTANTIVE INTRODUCTION

Africa's transitional political systems, their attendant instability, and frequent replacements of government elites make an interpretation of relations with foreign governments, particularly with Russia and China, difficult. Despite surface manifestations of similarities in foreign policy outlook and orientation between African and Socialist states, African nationalism is too potent a force to prostrate itself before a foreign ideology and to become Communist in the Soviet or Chinese sense. This does not mean, of course, that African states may not enter into instrumental alliances with Communist states, or that homegrown Communist groups may not turn international unrest into popular support.

When one examines the African experience in the past twenty-five years, however, this prospect appears unlikely. Of greater interest are certain individuals, with or without a national power base, in government circles in Africa who are self-proclaimed Marxists and who may influence their country's domestic and foreign policies. Thus far few such individuals have reached the Inner circles of government, and their impact has been minor. It is important to note that Russian interest in Africa has been declining and China's has been growing. Sub-Saharan Africa seems generally removed from immediate security needs and the mainstream of political and economic needs of both Moscow and Peking; but it is too early for long range judgments.

Western observers' views about Socialist states' foreign policy behavior in Africa have differed fundamentally from their views about other states. In general, the study of foreign policy has become more sophisticated and has attempted to analyze multiple elements (such as political, economic, military, strategic, cultural, psychological, domestic, and international determinants) whose importance in determining policy varies according to time, circumstance, or type of issue. By contrast, examinations of Communist policy toward Africa frequently posit a two-factor framework. This includes a powerful, all-encompassing and unyielding ideological framework, on one hand, and "normal" state interests on the other without, however, much differentiation of the elements of such interests. The latter interpretation assumes that the pursuit of national interests is appropriate because it conforms to accepted norms of behavior, but that ideology is not because it is aimed at world conquest or control at worst, or at transforming the globe into an environment favorably disposed toward communism at the very least.

The nature and distinctiveness of various Communist theories and ideological objectives create problems for the analyst. Concentration on ultimate aims may yield a "Communists will do no right" syndrome, whereas an emphasis on state policy may lead to a "don't bother me with fantasies" approach. Both these views are extreme, though not necessarily caricatures of tendencies in the literature.

Several factors explain the continued emphasis on the primacy of Communist ideological goals in the literature. It is simple to attack the rhetoric of Communist writers and the scope, the historical sweep, and the seemingly total commitment of official pronouncements. Analytic prudence, hostility to communism, and long-time intellectual conditioning also support this emphasis. Moreover, historical analogy may yield similar results; a few isolated voices which warned against the eventual dangers from Nazi Germany were correct, and the same arguments can be made cogently with respect to the dangers from communism.

No definitive answer can be given on whether ideology or national interest of Communist nations is stronger at this time. New approaches may be necessary to yield insights. Since in the Communist states behavior frequently deviates from ideological orthodoxy, the model may be adjusted to changing realities. The Communist states use only a fraction of their resources in Africa, so the actual potency of ideology is difficult to assess. Many western observers have adjusted their interpretations accordingly. One, in 1966, wrote that communism in Africa "is . . . a gigantic power-political compound . . . [for] securing total dominance of the whole world" (Schatten, COMMUNISM, p. 325). Another, writing two years earlier, stated that "it must . . . be recognized that Soviet state interests, and not the fortunes of communism, are the deciding factors" (Morison, U.S.S.R., p. 31). And a third, writing in 1974, suggested that "once the Western presence is removed, the next step will be to bring the African states into the Soviet orbit" (Klinghoffer, "Soviet Union," p. 77).

Clues to what motivates Communist states in Africa may be found in the writings of Soviet scholars specializing in Africa. Outsiders believe that many "contribute to the political goals of the state, and . . . confirm conclusions already established by . . . ideology" (Morris, "Soviet," p. 250), and thus emphasize not originality but conformity. Although by western standards Soviet research is of generally poor quality, additional examinations of it may produce more refined perceptions. One American observer believes that Soviet scholarship on Africa is a function of five factors; three derive from the nature of Russian involvement in Africa, one from the difficulties of coordinating policy with other socialist states, and a final one from the Soviet leadership system (Cohn, SOVIET POLICY). This scheme suggests differentiation

70

between kinds of domestic and external factors. Ironically, the quality of Soviet research on Africa has improved recently, probably because Africa now has a lower priority in the Kremlin.

Another factor affecting the behavior of Communist states in Africa may be those states' power positions in the world, particularly with regard to Russia and the People's Republic of China. The Soviet Union is a superpower with great economic and military muscle. Its vital concern is the prevention of nuclear war. The USSR can also afford to take global political, economic, and other initiatives while running only small risks. China, by contrast, is still a developing country, with only a small nuclear force. It is capable of playing a regional role in Asia but also apparently fears attack by either of the two superpowers. Whereas the Soviet Union views Africa from a position of strength, China sees Africa more as an equal. These reasons alone would be enough to create differences in the two countries' policies toward Africa. Western observers have suggested that in recent years Communist states have deemphasized ideology and stressed their national interests; ideology still counts as more than a mere ornament, but pragmatism in Africa predominates.

Most recent western observers believe that the Soviet Union has always considered Africa as subsidiary to other interests. This held true even in the brief period of the Khrushchev era, when Africa enjoyed greater status.

Soviet policy in Africa may be divided into two periods: the first under Lenin and Stalin, and the second under Khrushchev and his successors, coinciding roughly with the African states' independence. Africa had little importance during the first period. "These years of disregard," as one scholar put it, "compose the remarkably inauspicious prelude to the Soviet Union's clamoring entry into Africa" (Legvold, SOVIET POLICY, p. 2). During most of Lenin's life, Russia viewed colonial areas as instruments to bring about communism in Europe, predestined to be pressed into the service of the Russian revolution and the coming millenium. For this purpose Soviet doctrine counseled temporary alliances with bourgeois nationalists who were expected to bypass a capitalist stage of development. As prospects for the global revolution dimmed, Lenin sought a rapprochement with Europe. Since that policy could be jeopardized by courting Europe's African colonies, Russia's interest in Africa declined. Also, because Soviet expectations of mass uprisings which would lead to revolution proved to be too idealistic, the ideology shifted to envision Communist parties in the role of vanguards with the proper determination. But in practice, except for a highly unrealistic vision of a Communist South Africa, Russian leaders delegated their interests in Africa to European Communist parties. Except for some rhetoric, these parties were not notable for a defense of African interests. Consequently, Moscow gained no understanding of African nationalism. Instead, ignorance was added to misperception through secondhand information, a bit like trying to squint at a microbe through a fish eye lens.

When Europeans and Africans were exploring the possibility of fundamental changes in their relations, the Soviet outlook during the Stalin era seems to have been dominated by a rigid bipolar concept of the world and by inflated

estimates of European strength and resolve. The European colonies were regarded as reserves of the imperialist forces, and even after the achievement
of independence, it was recognized that colonial domination continued by other
means. The Soviet states looked at Africa as a vast, undifferentiated continent. They spoke of preferred developments which would take place in the
future and in two stages. First would come a stage of bourgeois democracy,
an interlude during which political developments would be guided by the big
African bourgeoisie basically supportive of the imperialist camp to which it
owed its prominence. The second stage was a true socialist revolution, hope-
fully led by a genuine proletariat that would eventually establish Soviet communism in the world.

The second period of Soviet policy toward Africa roughly covered the post-
independence era from 1958 to 1970 and involved three stages. From 1958
to 1960 came a stage of great optimism which was marked by selective support
for progressive African regimes and which can be illustrated by Soviet policy
toward Guinea. Soviets paid little heed to the independence of Ghana in
1957, chiefly because Russian leaders mistrusted Nkrumah, whom they regarded
as something short of a capitalist lackey. But the Russian leaders saw the political turbulence which accompanied Guinea's independence in 1958 as promising. Guinea's relations with France, and by extension with the West, were
severed abruptly, and President Toure vocally supported an African revolution.
Guinea was thus regarded as a sound prospect for moving toward the Socialist
camp because of its internal and foreign policy orientation, and Moscow began to cast a net in Africa. They established political and economic ties with
Guinea and then began to look for other likely prospects among African territories and states.

Soviet ideological changes in Africa during this first stage were guided from
above and initiated by Nikita Khrushchev, despite domestic opposition. Whereas
some saw these changes as bold achievements worthy of admiration, others believed that they represented adaptation of theory to newly perceived realities.
On the balance, they were more adaptation than bold innovation. To Moscow, it seemed that the world was taking a drastic turn which could be turned
to Russia's advantage. The 1955 Bandung conference of nonaligned nations
was an opportunity to weaken the grip of the western powers and eventually
alter the global balance of powers. The Soviets abandoned an earlier dislike
for nonalignment because they saw an opportunity to draw the nonaligned
states into the Socialist camp on the basis of a common antagonism toward
western imperialism. Also, a number of Third World countries had achieved,
or were about to achieve, political independence by peaceful means. This
meant that the ultimate solidification of the Socialist camp need not involve
violent revolution; instead, countries like Cuba and Guinea could be supported
with little risk and stand out as models of what the Third World could achieve
with the support of the Communists. Moreover, the Russians envisioned Guinea
as an opportunity to recuperate some lost prestige and to demonstrate the value
of Russian aid in competition with China's ideological militancy.

Russian support for Guinea was highly selective and to an extent it demonstrated

the lag between policy change and ideological reformulation. A monolithic
set of beliefs had lost some of its ability to serve as a rationalization for
policy. Tensions nevertheless remained between relatively catholic theory,
on one hand, and an actual policy based on clear and narrow ideological
preferences, on the other. The latter reflected the soaring post-Sputnik optimism in support of a great global socialist offensive.

Khrushchev insisted on a number of ideological adjustments during this period
of optimism. The Soviet Union "wanted allies rather than proselytes and in
this way [hoped] . . . to weaken the West" (Schatten, COMMUNISM, p. 97).
Cooperation with incumbent leadership in Africa and other developing countries
led to some theoretical reformulations. One was the new concept of the "national bourgeoisie"; this was simply a recognition that incumbent elites were
more appropriate as contacts than the revolutionary underground, since the
former were in office. Local Communist parties did not seem promising, so
the Soviet Union simply conferred legitimacy on existing African leaders.
Moreover, in the absence of genuine proletarian leadership, national bourgeois
leaders were believed capable of moving toward noncapitalist development, if
not toward authentic socialism.

The Soviets also abandoned their bitter denunciations of African socialism.
The concept of socialism posed a serious problem for Russia, because it stressed
African distinctiveness and separateness and suggested a way toward utopia
different from that officially sanctioned. Given the popularity of socialism in
Africa, suggestions by Russia that it be abandoned and replaced by "real" socialism would have been useless. Hence, Moscow no longer insisted on the sanc-
tity of its own dogma and instead adapted its theory to African preferences.
The new policy held that there were many paths to socialism and implied that
neither Communist parties nor well defined stages toward the revolution were
essential—at least in Africa. The image of African states as imperialist reserves gradually disappeared, and the states were defined as deserving of Russian
support as part of the great worldwide Socialist offensive. Thus, during the
Khrushchev phase of Soviet policy toward Africa, Russia increased its influence
in Africa, tailoring some of its ideology for that purpose, but it remained selective in its African contacts.

The second stage of Russian involvement in Africa after independence lasted
approximately from 1960 to 1963. The Soviets' optimistic views about the expansion of the worldwide Socialist offensive persisted, and they hoped Russia
would become the chief counselor of the new states. African independence
was viewed not as an eruption of political sovereignty but as the surface mani-
festation of a more fundamental movement. The bitter divisions among two
groups of African states suggested that political independence did not automati-
cally imply anti-imperialist leanings. But Moscow persistently supported the
Casablanca group and excoriated most moderate and conservative states.

Russia supported the Mali Republic and later Ghana because the Kremlin viewed
these states as favorable for cooperation. It marked the beginning of discrimi-

nation of individual African states in the abstraction of Africa. Nkrumah had a new team of advisers supportive of the Socialist states and was frustrated at the United Nations' actions in the Congo. The Mali Republic was fearful of isolation and was willing to experiment with domestic political and economic structures. The turning of attention toward Ghana and Mali may also have been caused by Russia's clumsy handling of the situation in Guinea and that country's stiff reaction against Moscow in the name of African nationalism. Rapidly changing events in Africa eroded the bases for ideologically determined policy.

The third stage of Russia's Africa policy began around 1963 as a result of two developments: a Soviet reevaluation of the importance of Third World countries in general and the creation of the Organization of African Unity, with the accompanying realization that Africa was different from the Kremlin's image of it. The developing states, upon which Russian leaders had counted as part of an anti-imperialist movement, turned out to behave as independent countries unwilling to be manipulated by outsiders for alien causes, and thus their importance was downgraded. Soviet leaders turned to a new, low-profile policy designed to diversify their relations without strong emphasis on ideology.

After Khrushchev, Soviet policy turned toward pragmatism and conservatism. Attempting to apply Communist ideology to Africa had turned policy into an endlessly frustrating obstacle course. Russian diplomats in Africa have been quoted as privately expressing surprise that Europeans were able to deal with Africans for so long--a testimonial to their frustration in finding that Africa that did not conform to their prior images. The new all-African organization also suggested that Russia would be better served by adapting to Africa on African terms. Soviet statements became pessimistic in assessing African stability and prospects for economic growth, and Russia's advice about self-reliance and diversification of external support came to resemble that of western nations. Russia therefore initiated normal interstate relations with Africa and also pursued Soviet interests as they emerged in competition with Peking and Chinese activities in the Middle East and the Indian Ocean.

As are the United States and the Soviet Union, the People's Republic of China is a recent newcomer to Africa. China's policy toward Africa can be divided into two phases, one lasting for the first fifteen years after the Bandung conference and another since then. Chinese policy was determined by domestic factors--including political and economic turbulence, isolation and hence ignorance of Africa, and ideological predilections--as well as by external events-- China's position in the world system and competition with Russia. Chinese policy generally has been cautious and pragmatic, though the Chinese have suffered from misconceptions and have made some serious errors of judgment.

In the years during and after Bandung, which provided China with partial entree into the international state system, Peking did not regard Africa as important. China's policy at first developed along similar lines as Russian policy. With Russia, China shared illusions and excessive optimism about Third World development. Chinese policy for Africa showed no clear overall goals during

74

the first period, and many actions reflected ad hoc decision making. During this period Chinese policy suffered from false expectations, extraordinary caution combined with ill-devised sudden forays, rising frustrations at Soviet inroads, disappointment at lack of African cooperation, and failure to influence Africa on numerous important issues. To many African leaders the People's Republic was an unknown entity, not without attractive features but still unfamiliar. By contrast, many Africans were accustomed to useful cooperation with the Republic of China.

Peking began to play a more independent role in Africa once China's relations with Russia deteriorated, but China's experience in Africa was less than glorious. Chou En-lai's visit to Africa in late 1963 and early 1964 signified a more active policy and a challenge to the Soviets. At that time Chinese leaders offered their own model for world revolution but also bypassed Communist parties for cooperation with incumbent African regimes where appropriate. To distinguish itself from major powers (chiefly Russia) whose influence and overtures were suspect, China emphasized self-reliance for Africa and projected itself as another developing nation whose successes were relevant to the new African states. Nevertheless, Africa was a low priority for Peking. During the second (1964) Congo crisis, for example, the Chinese gave symbolic material support for rebels who controlled half that country's territory and who were ideologically close to communism. Objective conditions were such that "the situation is favorable but the leadership is weak" (Larkin, CHINA, p. 56).

The Chinese political, as distinct from economic and social, revolutionary model has thus far had limited appeal for Africans. Despite some advantages of the model's strategic and tactical flexibility, the Chinese have warned prospective followers not to copy it blindly. This caution many have resulted from earlier Chinese experiences in Asia, where it proved difficult to export and duplicate.

The model consists of three parts: (1) a revolutionary Communist party, whose role is one of leadership in deciding policy and controlling structures, (2) the armed forces, to be used as needed to support the Party, and (3) the United Front, a notion, according to one critic, so vague as to "border on fiction" (Larkin, CHINA, p. 151). It is a device to attract and unify those elements of the population willing to make common cause with the aims of the Party and is thus a symbol of broad popular support. The relation among the three parts is dynamic rather than static, and it reflects the Communists' domestic experience in their long struggle for supremacy. It places great emphasis on tactical flexibility (retreat and/or advance as deemed prudent or necessary) and on an image of a city encircled by the country (at the global level, the highly industrialized capitalist states being slowly encircled by the much larger, rural Third World).

The model's prescriptions, along with the Chinese admonitions for patience, have some appeal, since they are practical and are based on the conviction of eventual victory. But the model seems to appeal most to those who have little to lose, especially groups thoroughly alienated from their national society, as in either independent black Africa or in southern Africa. Chinese prescriptions are intended to "achieve ambitious goals in a hostile setting and with meagre means, by an apt combination of political and military struggle" (Larkin, CHINA, p. 152).

In the African setting the Chinese model for revolution suffers from significant handicaps. The sponsoring of international, African-Chinese pressure groups, involving people as diverse as gymnasts and scientists, for instance, as part of a united front against imperialism competes with the socialization and political mobilization efforts of incumbent governments. Amid the many African military regimes it would be difficult to argue the merits of civilian or party supremacy over the armed forces. African armed forces often dislike the political process and attempt to sidetrack or muzzle political parties. African civilian regimes think of their armed forces as defensive, symbolic, and civic-action oriented, and they have not enlisted them in armed struggle against colonialism and imperialism. Creation of Communist parties in Africa may conflict with nationalism which requires that political parties be indigenous in orientation and free from external control; they could also endanger Chinese objectives by becoming involved in the Sino-Soviet dispute. That dispute has arisen in Africa on many occasions and has drawn fire from African leaders, who contend that they have enough problems of their own and who insist that Russians and Chinese fight their battles elsewhere.

It is probably too early to judge China's future policy in Africa. China's universal diplomatic recognition has had no apparent effect, and what change there has been--some increased activity--can be ascribed to normal state behavior as well as to ideological beliefs on the part of Peking's leaders. No doubt the dramatic change from pariah to valuable member of the international community will increase China's leverage abroad. Partly because of lack of information and the relatively brief period of its involvement, China's objectives in Africa can only be divined. One recent student distinguishes between short-term and long-term goals in an effort to come to grips with this problem (Larkin, CHINA). He suggests that long-range goals are visionary and idealistic and flow from doctrine. Stated long-range goals include a global social revolution and a universal "cultural revolution" which recasts men's minds and helps create an international environment presumed to be devoid of dangers for China. This outlook, and the rhetoric which it issues, have the inherent advantage of being in harmony with some of Africa's stated long-range goals. China will thus "contribute to thoughts about proper world order circulating in Africa and to the repertoire of revolutionary expectations and techniques" (Larkin, CHINA, p. 6).

China's short-term objectives relate to the Sino-Soviet dispute, the need for recognition, and the desire to extend its influence. No doubt China's future African policy will be watched carefully to discover if there is an inverse relationship between long- and short-range goals: the more short-term and evolutionary goals are achieved, the less concern there is for long-range and revolutionary goals. It must be assumed, however, that China is in Africa to stay.

Socialist Countries and Africa

Present relations with and commitments to Africa will probably take on importance in their own right, and it would be unreasonable to expect China to abandon them. It may be that China's path to revolution, based chiefly on domestic experience, will continue to be of limited applicability elsewhere. But her influence in Africa, in the more conventional sense, likely will grow.

Since 1954, when Communist states began economic development assistance programs for developing countries (1956 for the People's Republic of China), total commitments by 1972 reached about $15 billion. The bulk was made available to the Middle East and South Asia, with about 15 percent earmarked for Africa. Obligations for 1972 illustrate some significant aspects of the Communists' aid program. In that year new pledges came to $1.7 billion for all recipients, slightly lower than the 1971 total of $1.8 billion. Most of the commitments were again made to the Middle East and to South Asia. Of the 1972 total Eastern Europe accounted for 37 percent, Russia's share was down to one-third ($580 million), and China's was $500 million.

Continental Africa's share of total Communist aid to developing countries has been increasing. Although it actually dropped from 35 percent in 1971 to 24 percent in 1972, this needs to be compared with 15 percent of the total since the inception of aid programs. Much of this shift in the relative priority of Africa is accounted for by the increase in Chinese contributions, which have risen noticeably since 1970. China's commitments to the African continent represent 18 percent of all Chinese aid, but it accounted for nearly half of all Communist aid to Africa by 1972. This dramatic increase reflected Chinese commitments for the building of the Tanzania-Zambia (TanZam) railroad, the largest single aid project funded by a Communist country in a developing state, for which nearly $500 million were earmarked by 1970, out of a cumulative total of $1.1 billion for Africa. Other recipients of substantial Communist aid obligations in sub-Saharan Africa in 1971 and 1972 included the Sudan ($115 million from Eastern Europe and China), Somalia ($110 million from China), Ethiopia ($85 million from China), and Zambia ($50 million from Eastern Europe).

As is true with western aid, that from Communist states is also highly concentrated. In 1972, for instance, Soviet aid went to five developing states—none in Africa; Eastern European pledges were made to eleven states, including four in the African continent; Chinese commitments were made to fourteen developing countries, including six in Africa. Communist aid is generally given on liberal financial terms, although only about half the total, cumulative commitments were drawn by 1972. Nearly all aid is in the form of loans, for which China requires no interest and Russia and Eastern Europe ask for between 2.5 percent and 3.5 percent interest, to be repaid in one or two decades. Communist assistance is also generally tied to the purchase of goods and services in donor countries.

In addition to financial assistance, Communist states send technical experts to and train students from developing countries. The African continent was host to 70 percent of the 90,000 technical assistance personnel from Communist states.

More than 90 percent of all Chinese experts were in Africa, related chiefly to the TanZam railroad. Students attending academic institutions in Communist countries made up half the worldwide total of 24,000 in 1972. Nigeria and the Sudan stood out for having sent more than 1,000 students each. In 1972 China accepted the first group of students since 1966, so that almost all such students thus far have been trained in Russia and Eastern Europe.

Most military aid to developing countries from Communist states comes from the Soviet Union. Russian military aid between 1955 and 1972 totaled $8.5 billion, of which only $205 million went to sub-Saharan Africa ($400 million went to Algeria alone). Of the twelve states of sub-Saharan Africa which have recently benefited from Russian military supplies, only Somalia and the Sudan received more than $50 million in that seventeen-year period. It is believed that none, or very few, of the 28,000 military personnel from the developing states being trained in Russia came from Africa. Furthermore, few of the Soviet military personnel stationed in developing areas were thought to be in sub-Saharan Africa, except for Somalia, although there have been press reports of Russian military involvement in Guinea as part of Russia's support for the liberation of Portuguese Guinea.

Trade between Communist and developing countries has grown slowly.[2] Total turnover (exports and imports) rose from $4.5 billion in 1967 to $6.2 billion in 1971, a 5 percent increase over the previous year. The relative importance of this trade to both categories of partners remains small. The Communist countries' share of total developing areas' turnover reached 4.7 percent for exports and 5.1 percent for imports in 1971. The corresponding importance of Communist states for developing countries was somewhat greater and varied considerably, with the developing countries' total turnover share being 20 percent for China, about 10 percent for the Soviet Union, and 6 percent for Eastern Europe.

Of the total trade between developing and Communist states, the continent of Africa accounted for 18 percent in 1971. Chinese trade with developing countries, Africa included, has been rising fastest. Significant trade nonetheless remained concentrated on a few countries. Trade between Communist states and sub-Saharan Africa rose from $665 million in 1970 to $790 million the next year. Trade with Communist countries does not represent a large proportion of the external trade relations of African states. In 1971 the Communist states' share of exports in Africa represented only a few percentage points, and was near or above 10 percent only in Togo (13.5 percent) and the Sudan (32 percent); corresponding figures for imports were similar, with only three countries above the 10 percent mark. (Angola and Mozambique registered some

---

2. For details, consult COMMUNIST STATES AND DEVELOPING COUNTRIES: AID AND TRADE IN 1972. Washington, D.C.: Department of State, Bureau of Intelligence and Research, RECS-10, June 15, 1973.

of the smallest percentages in Africa.)

A review of the data on commercial relations between Africa and Communist states suggests that, once established, they do not change significantly. Communist states are increasingly willing to trade with moderate African states. Most Socialist countries buy chiefly mineral and agricultural products and sell machinery and equipment. The structure of these trade relations thus resembles that of western and other developed nations and is generally a function of elements of economic complementarity rather than ideological considerations.

B. THE SOVIET UNION AND EASTERN EUROPE

183 Ayih, Michel. EIN AFRIKANER IN MOSKAU. Cologne, West Germany: Bertlesmann, 1961. 196 p.

> The story of a Togolese student who attended an international youth festival in Moscow and returned as a student to Lomonosov University for two years. His initial curiosity turned to apprehension and then shock at the suspicions, regimentation, political indoctrination, prejudice, and government investigations which he and his friends encountered.

184 Cohn, Helen Desfosses. SOVIET POLICY TOWARD BLACK AFRICA: THE FOCUS ON NATIONAL INTEGRATION. New York: Praeger, 1972. 270 p. Bibliography.

> A detailed review of the evolution of Russian thought on such questions as African nationalism and its role regarding anti-imperialism, African national integration, political problems, economic progress, and social groups. Paying particular attention to the role of Russian scholars, the author suggests that students of Africa now have greater freedom to stray from ideological and political constraints than previously, but that this may stem from Africa's lack of importance to Soviet leaders.

185 Hamrell, Sven, and Widstrand, Carl Goesla, eds. THE SOVIET BLOC, CHINA AND AFRICA. Uppsala, Sweden: Scandinavian Institute of African Studies, 1964. 158 p. Paperback.

> Essays representing early efforts by western scholars to understand such topics as pan-Africanism, Soviet and Chinese policy, the influence of communism, and the Sino-Soviet split and their relation to independent Africa.

186 Kanet, Roger E. "The Soviet Union and the Colonial Question, 1917-1953 and Soviet Attitudes Since Stalin." In his THE SOVIET UNION AND THE DEVELOPING NATIONS, pp. 1-50. Baltimore: Johns Hopkins University Press, 1974.

A detailed study which shows that Russian thinking has moved
away from Lenin's thoughts on imperialism. Increasingly drawn
to pragmatic adjustment of even fundamental tenets of official
ideology, Russia has adapted to the changing world environment
and is now inclined to follow new opportunities to strengthen
her national interests while preserving ideological "consistency"
through mental gyrations.

187   Klinghoffer, Arthur Jay. SOVIET PERSPECTIVES ON AFRICAN SOCIAL-
ISM. Teaneck, N.J.: Fairleigh Dickinson University Press, 1969. 248 p.
Bibliography.

A thorough examination of the changes in Russian views about
Africa from Stalin to Khrushchev, with particular attention to
the African version of socialism and some key Soviet components
like the class struggle and society and to expectations about
Africa's transition toward scientific socialism. Early expectations eventually yielded to practical experience and required
drastic adjustments. This situation is comparable to the evolution of France's assimilation policy.

188   _____. "The Soviet Union and Africa." In THE SOVIET UNION AND
THE DEVELOPING NATIONS, edited by Roger E. Kanet, pp. 51-77.
Baltimore: Johns Hopkins University Press, 1974.

A brief review of Soviet policy beginning with Khrushchev,
whose aggressive foreign policy behavior led to his removal
from office. The author finds that Russia's chief aim in Africa
remains the expansion of its influence to "bring the African
states into the Soviet orbit."

189   Legvold, Robert. SOVIET POLICY IN WEST AFRICA. Cambridge, Mass.:
Harvard University Press, 1969. 348 p.

A competent and well written study which reviews Soviet policy
from before World War II until 1968. The chronological framework has the advantage of easy tracing of the Russian leaders'
adjustment to newly perceived realities. Krushchev's experimen-
tation and the subsequent sharp drop of Russian interest, plus
the growing competition with China, are highlights of this period.

190   Morison, David. THE U.S.S.R. AND AFRICA. London: Oxford University Press, for the Royal Institute of Race Relations and the Central
Asian Research Center, 1964. 74 p. Appendix, paperback.

A primer, though necessarily somewhat dated, on Soviet objectives and attitudes, on the state of African studies in Russia,
and on significant differences of views among Soviet observers.

191 Morris, Milton D. "The Soviet Africa Institute and the Development
of African Studies." JOURNAL OF MODERN AFRICAN STUDIES 11
(June 1973): 247–65.

Whereas American Africanists take pride in their independence
from government policy and are among that policy's most vocal
critics, their Soviet counterparts, according to this article, are
less privileged and "expected to contribute to the political
goals of the State." The noticeable improvement in the quality
of Soviet work results from greater freedom as the importance
of Africa has declined for policy makers. However, they need
basic information to complement a Russian policy shift toward
development problems.

192 Schatten, Fritz. COMMUNISM IN AFRICA. New York: Praeger,
1966. 343 p.

A compendium written by an East German refugee with no particular love for communism. This book traces the many efforts
by international communism, both Russian and Chinese, to in-
filtrate Africa and influence the future.

193 Stokke, Baard Richard. SOVIET AND EAST EUROPEAN TRADE AND
AID IN AFRICA. New York: Praeger, 1967. 295 p. Tables, bibliography.

A detailed study of trade and aid in the decade ending in 1966,
specific relations with twelve African states, and of likely future developments. The Russians and their East European friends
have learned from their early mistakes and, the author states,
African leaders have become less naive.

C. THE PEOPLE'S REPUBLIC OF CHINA

194 Cooley, John K. EAST WIND OVER AFRICA: RED CHINA'S AFRICAN
OFFENSIVE. New York: Walker, 1965. 220 p. Appendices.

A fast-paced, somewhat gloomy account by a CHRISTIAN SCI-
ENCE MONITOR correspondent of myriad Chinese activities in
Africa and the dangers these contain. The book suggests that,
although complete domination of Africa is not now (1965) the
aim of China, Africa is nonetheless important to China in relation to intermediate Third World and domestic objectives and
will grow in importance.

195 Hevi, John Emmanuel. THE DRAGON'S EMBRACE: THE CHINESE
COMMUNISTS AND AFRICA. New York: Praeger, 1966. 137 p.
Appendices, illustrations.

An account written by a Ghanaian after he spent two years as

a student in China. He has a dominant commitment to African
independence, and this book suggests that "China's intentions
in Africa cannot possibly be in the best interests of us Africans."

196 Larkin, Bruce D. CHINA AND AFRICA, 1949-1970: THE FOREIGN
POLICY OF THE PEOPLE'S REPUBLIC OF CHINA. Berkeley and Los
Angeles: University of California Press, 1971. 212 p. Appendix,
bibliographic note, bibliography.

A thoughtful and provocative study. The author reviews chronological background of Chinese involvement, economic ties, liberation movements, and Chinese failures, but emphasizes the
importance and nature of Chinese doctrine and some of the
difficulties in evaluating it as a determinant of policy. He
provides a necessary corrective to lesser accounts and suggests
that, whereas China will probably not achieve its revolutionary
ideal, there are many circumstances which may well propitiate
significantly greater Chinese influence in Africa.

197 Slawecki, Leon M.S. "The Two Chinas and Africa." FOREIGN AF-
FAIRS 41 (January 1963): 398-409.

A detailed examination of the efforts by the Republic of China and
the People's Republic of China to seek influence in Africa, of their
respective assets, and of the African states' early response.

198 Tareq, Ismael Y. "The People's Republic of China and Africa." JOUR-
NAL OF MODERN AFRICAN STUDIES 9 (December 1971): 507-29.

A review of the evolution of China's motivations and efforts
to establish African contacts. Peking's policies are seen as a
function of the dispute with Russia, of policies in Asia and the
Middle East, of conditions in southern Africa, and of adaptation to a better understanding of African needs.

Chapter 5

AFRICAN LIBERATION MOVEMENTS

A. SUBSTANTIVE INTRODUCTION

Most of the attention shown by scholars to conflicts which oppose African liberation movements to incumbent governments and elites has focused on southern Africa and Guinea-Bissau. Much of the discussion, often cast in moral absolutes, has preached only to the converted and has sustained preestablished elements of faith. The result has been little more than a dialog of the deaf, whose participants are unwilling to listen to one another.

For more than a decade until April 1974 the governments of South Africa, Rhodesia, and Portugal contended that the black freedom fighters operating in these countries were illegitimate by definition. These governments portrayed liberation movements as small bands of chronic, inconsequential malcontents pursuing selfish interests. Liberationists were seen as troublemakers who operated at the expense of their peoples, duped by heady but false myths of international communism into lawless behavior indirectly threatening the existence of western and/or white civilization. Hence they were viewed as a threat to sovereign domestic affairs beyond the jurisdiction of misguided foreign states and ill-disposed international organizations. Such arguments have justified impressive outlays and sacrifices for national defense, which have further been supported by the liberation movements' relative ineffectiveness in the field.

Insurgent groups, in contrast, operate at different levels of reality. They argue in terms of sacred rights to self-determination and majority rule. They object to the systematic repression of peaceful protest, the banning of embryonic and peaceful political parties, the restricting of educational and social opportunities, and the total blocking of channels for meaningful participation and change. Moreover, they object to the facts that white minorities protect their social and economic rewards against the nonwhite majorities which they govern and that the whites find it difficult to abandon feelings of superiority which characterized the recent colonial era. Hence, liberation movements can make sacrifices and undergo hardships designed to bring about human justice, of which their members have been deprived.

Ironically, both sides make demands on western powers, although for entirely different reasons. These demands may result from implicit notions that western powers bear a large measure of responsibility for solving the conflict, that they are the effective powers in the international state system, and that they are supporters of fundamental justice and legitimacy. Both sides also denounce western powers, however, either for duplicity or for failure to support the parties to the fullest.

In this kind of conflict logic may envenom rather than smooth relations. The search for logical consistency often merely confirms that the other fellow is a hypocrite and perpetuates comfortable fictions and stereotypes. African leaders and western observers sometimes interpret the reluctance of western powers to become involved as an indication that these countries have abandoned universal standards of justice, or that they favor, directly or indirectly, the continuation of white supremacy and racist exploitation. Western powers have also been taken to task for differential responses to gross violations of basic human rights. Internal disturbances in independent black-ruled African states have generally produced silence or indifference on the part of the international state systems. The great wall of silence which prevented effective international concern, African and foreign, for such tragedies as attempts by black Sudanese to liberate themselves from northern domination, or the massacres in Burundi in which hundreds of thousands of Africans were killed by Africans, contrasts sharply with the quick uproar generated by the shooting of sixty-nine Africans by panicky police in South Africa. These responses are a sad commentary on the selectivity with which the international system responds to human tragedy.

The conflict in southern Africa revolves around the determination to maintain white supremacy regimes, on one hand, and the swelling demands for self-determination and majority rule, on the other. What logical purists tend to overlook is that the international state system recognizes conflicting standards of behavior as legitimate. International concern for questions of human rights, self-determination, and racial discrimination is as legitimate as the defense of sovereign states against subversion and terrorism. If the conventions of the international system allow contradictory behavior, then logical consistency is unlikely to be crucial; both Bangladesh and Biafra claimed the right of self-determination in their secession attempt, but the principle had little to do with the outcome.

Discussion of this conflict will not advance far without reference to another phenomenon: the dominant commitment of the age to end colonialism, minimally defined as direct political control by minorities perceived as foreign by the majorities, a process commonly referred to as "decolonization." This widespread commitment is irreversible and is sanctified by international convention; Africa will not rest until it is achieved. This is the crux of the conflict in southern Africa.

The desire to change existing political conditions in South Africa is the same as in the rest of Africa. There have been brief and at times bloody wars of resistance by Africans, who were overwhelmed by technologically superior

Europeans. In recent years Africans have had greater exposure to political and social ideals denied them in their own land. Restiveness has increased as people no longer believed that existing conditions were inevitable. What set southern Africa and Portuguese Guinea apart was the incumbent governments' unwillingness to permit the decolonization process from proceeding. Consequently, in South Africa and to a lesser degree Rhodesia, there are dangerous accumulated frustrations with alien elites whose official policy perpetuates not only political domination but also social and economic opportunities based on racial criteria. In the former Portuguese territories, such conflicts were often less severe because of Portugal's more relaxed attitude on racial and humanitarian issues. Most observers nonetheless agree that, since significant channels for change were obstructed, there was no alternative to violence.

Dissident movements and actual or potential guerilla fighters are found in other places as well as in southern Africa and Guinea-Bissau. The existence of such groups elsewhere in Africa reflects the syncretic nature of the emerging African societies, which are encased in new political boundaries with a low level of national identification. One student provides a simple typology of African liberation movements by using the two broad categories of, first, objectives and, second, techniques and bases of support (Grundy, GUERILLA, pp. 75-78). He singles out four kinds of goals: (1) independence from colonial (white) regimes (the Portuguese territories); (2) majority rule from alien regimes (South Africa, South West Africa, and Rhodesia); (3) secession from or autonomy in indigenous black African regimes (the Eritrean Liberation Front in Ethiopia, the former Anya'nya in the Sudan, or the Biafrans); and (4) revolution against independent black regimes (Chad or Burundi). He distinguishes between traditional and modern, illustrated by the Mau Mau or Mulelists as traditional, and most other insurgent groups, which are modern at least in orientation.

Such analytical distinctions are imprecise, but they are useful because they focus on fundamental assumptions about the success and legitimacy of liberation movements in Africa. First, national and modern groups are believed to have a better chance for success because of the nature of politics in transition toward modernization. Second, movements which fight for majority rule and/or independence from incumbent elites considered to be external to Africa are widely considered legitimate. And third, those fighting for secession, autonomy, rebellion, or even majority rule in states already under black African political control, are frequently seen as illegitimate. The reasons for these classifications can be found in the present international and domestic political climate in Africa. Forcible change in existing political frontiers is considered too dangerous, because it might invite emulation and bring about political and territorial chaos throughout Africa, since states do not follow the many ethnic divisions. Presumably, the end of colonial domination by white regimes carries no such threat.

African liberation movements can be classified also by target country. Thus, one student lists fifteen major and seven minor movements in ten target areas, and another scholar identifies fifteen movements in nine countries (Gibson, LIBERATION; and Grundy, GUERILLA).

85

Significant liberation movements have been active in southern Africa (South Africa, South West Africa, Rhodesia, and the Portuguese areas of Angola and Mozambique), the Spanish-controlled Canary Islands in the Atlantic Ocean, the French territory of the Afar and Issa (Djibouti) at the mouth of the Red Sea, and in many independent African states such as Chad, Ethiopia, and the Sudan.

Most liberation movements have received their basic support from one or two ethnic groups in the target territory, and, in most cases, these groups are a minority of the total African population in the area. Also, there are at least two rival movements in each of the target areas in southern Africa and in Guinea-Bissau. In some cases, one group has emerged as the more effective, has managed to dominate international headlines and external support, and has made the best preparations for eventual independence. Such preparations go beyond the development of an effective fighting force and include provision of social and educational services and political recruitment and indoctrination-- in other words, the groundwork for the new independent state. Finally, the bitter disputes between Russia and China, the Sino-Soviet split, have affected African liberation movements by reinforcing existing divisions between and inside such movements, within and outside the target area. Although it is difficult to suggest any cause and effect relationship, the Russian-supported liberation movements have relatively better educated leadership, tend to be urban in outlook, and multiracial; by contrast, those supported by Peking have leadership groups which are less well educated, uniracial (black) in outlook, and rural or urban proletarian in origin.

Most of these movements would not survive without external support. There are two sources for such support: one is the independent African states, which channel their contributions through the Organization of African Unity's African Liberation Committee (ALC), and the other is external to Africa. Support consists mostly of financial and material aid, but also of diplomatic and political activities.

Financial assistance from the ALC is marginal. The OAU is not a supra-national organization, and the ALC merely coordinates what help is provided by sovereign independent states. Extra-African sources prefer to channel their aid bilaterally. Liberation movements consider themselves autonomous, and they are not always amenable to ALC coordination efforts in political or military activities. Africans have criticized the ALC frequently for alleged ineptitude and mismanagement of funds. Some of this criticism may be politically inspired because the committee has been dominated by "radical" states. But one crucial problem is the gap between the promised budget, based on assessed contributions by OAU members, and actual appropriations. Hard budgetary information is notoriously inaccurate and is not made public. The 1973 ALC budget request was reportedly for $3.5 million, a 100 percent increase over the previous year.[3]

---

3. Cf. Yashpal Tandon, "The Organization of African Unity and the Liberation of Southern Africa," in Potholm, SOUTHERN AFRICA, pp. 254-55; and AFRICA RESEARCH BULLETIN: POLITICAL, SOCIAL, AND CULTURAL SERIES 10 (June 15, 1973): 2844C.

ALC strategy in recent years has concentrated aid on the Portuguese areas. Another important element of ALC help is its recognition policy. Official recognition criteria include (1) demonstrated success in the field, (2) unification of rival movements in the same territory, and (3) the vague notion of general reliability. Only the first of these has been the operative criterion however, and the message is "nothing succeeds like success." Perhaps by coincidence, most ALC support has gone to movements favored by the Soviet Union.

African states known to contribute most to guerillas are those contiguous to target areas, although Algeria's revolutionary experience has also been attractive to liberation movements. The remainder of Africa contributes according to ability and domestic priorities. As might be expected, a geographic location next to a target area can pose serious problems, and the willingness of such states to bear such burdens is testimony to their commitment to speed the decolonization process. Another problem results from refugees, who at the date of this writing number about half a million. Refugees can be divided into two groups, those who fled the fighting and are not necessarily committed to armed struggle and those who are political refugees or belong to guerilla groups. In the early 1960s, most refugees belonged to ethnic groups which crossed political frontiers, and they were usually integrated into the new country. International organizations have aided the subsequent massive influxes of refugees. Host countries, having only limited resources, have mostly abandoned their initial welcome in favor of more restrictive policies.

Another problem involves guerilla recruitment among refugees. Guerilla forces occasionally come into physical conflict with one another, which requires intervention by the host country. There is also a delicate question of control over guerilla fighting forces, which may have more men under arms than the host country has in its regular armed forces and police units. At times guerillas undertake military activities against the best interests of the host government, such as sabotage of external transportation links which are economically crucial. Finally, the presence of guerillas poses external dangers. Host countries must therefore walk a thin line between support for liberation movements and avoidance of excessive antagonism from target countries. There have been numerous reports of hot pursuit attacks on land and in the air by Portugal and other white-controlled regimes in western and southern Africa, involving such countries as Senegal and Zambia. Host countries are sanctuaries where insurgents can rest and hide, but target forces will penetrate for reprisals. Host countries need to deploy their meager armed forces to border areas, removing them from places where they may be needed for internal security.

Extra-African sources of assistance for guerilla fighters include, in order of descending importance (1) the socialist countries, notably the Soviet Union and the People's Republic of China but also Eastern Europe, (2) some western countries—Sweden, for instance, makes annual appropriations for health and educational services, and (3) some international organizations like the World Council of Churches, which in 1972 made available $100,000 and pledged to increase that amount in subsequent years. These sources contribute about 90 percent of the aid flowing to African liberation movements. Among the eleven active liberation movements in southern Africa, the Soviet Union is the principal source of financial and material aid for five and the People's Republic of China for five others. In 1973 the OAU decided to send missions abroad to secure funds, and the priorities indicate their expectations. Missions were to visit Socialist states, nonaligned states for a show of solidarity, and some sympathetic western states in Scandinavia. The omission of most western states merely indicates that request for support from them was regarded as futile. The United Nations and its specialized agencies have also given vocal support to the cause of decolonization, particularly to the guerilla struggle in southern Africa and Portuguese Guinea. The many UN resolutions on that topic, the expulsion of South Africa from UN organs, and actions taken on South West Africa, Guinea-Bissau, and Rhodesia have swayed world public opinion and tended to isolate the colonial regimes and given hope to freedom fighters in these areas.

Attempts at coordination among liberation movements have been unsuccessful. Most do meet at international conferences and some have joined common roof organizations, but these alliances seem ineffective. Some such conferences sponsored or dominated by the Russians or Chinese deepened the divisions among the African participants. Moreover, cooperation among different liberation movements in the field have not been very successful. Such attempts have involved alliances or joint action as a means of gaining access to target areas. In 1967 and 1968, for instance, the African National Congress of South Africa entered into such an alliance with Rhodesia's Zimbabwe African National Union (ZANU); the South African contingent hoped to penetrate farther south, and ZANU wanted to strike a blow in Rhodesia. The freedom fighters were intercepted, and the attempt proved counterproductive, for it triggered the participation of South African police units in the defense of Rhodesia and the cooperation of Portuguese authorities to help prevent further incursions. In addition, repeated mediation efforts by the OAU and individual African statesmen between guerilla groups in the same territory produced only paper agreements and did not affect basic divisions.

The incumbent regimes of southern Africa, by contrast, were united in their objective to maintain the status quo, at least until the 1974 military coup d'etat replaced the Portuguese government. To maintain the status quo, they have overcome animosities of long-standing, like those based on racial distinctions (Afrikaners and British vs. Latin Portuguese), religion (Protestant vs. Roman Catholic), general outlook concerning human relations (apartheid vs. multiracialism), and on self-esteem factors relating to their capabilities to handle their respective insurgent groups. Cooperation is well established on issues such as the exchange of intelligence and select military consultation and support. Their predisposition to band together and to protect what they consider their national interests need not be formalized; as South African Prime Minister John Vorster expressed it: "We are good friends . . . and good friends do not need a pact. Good friends know what their duty is if a neighbour's house is on fire" (Quoted in Grundy, CONFRONTATION, p. 133).

Unlike the liberation movements, the incumbent governments have the means to buy what they need and are more self-sufficient and have vastly superior armed forces. South Africa is self-reliant in small arms. All three regimes have been able to secure additional, sophisticated military hardware through direct or circuitous business transactions, mostly with European countries or private suppliers. International bans, boycotts, and understandings designed to deny these countries weapons for anti-guerilla warfare have been evaded with relative ease.

Most observers sympathize with the cause of decolonization and liberation movements in southern Africa and existing economic and other ties between the three target countries and western powers, particularly the United States, have been severely criticized. Much of such criticism rests on moral grounds, suggesting that normal relations with these regimes is equivalent to complicity in repression against freedom fighters. Some critics have focused on a quantitative enumeration of existing economic and military ties and have suggested that these contribute to the target regimes' abilities to resist change. It is not entirely clear to what extent these "contributions" are responsible for policy, however, since critics address questions of incremental capability rather than of determination and intent. What seems clear is that, without determination, the target regimes would become amenable to a political rather than a military solution.

The possibility of direct involvement in southern Africa by western powers has received wide discussion. Intervention is sometimes seen as a logical extension of present commitments in the area or as a pattern of such involvement elsewhere in the Third World. Kenneth W. Grundy wrote that "the more the Communist states assist African revolutionaries, the more the Western states and NATO—judging from past performance—will feel obliged to prop up the minority white government" (CONFRONTATION, p. 224). Others use the specter of direct western military involvement as an instrument to frighten their audience away from present ties. These ties should be severed now, lest the region become another Vietnam or lead to an American-Russian or American-Chinese confrontation and court racial unrest in the United States.

These views may be questioned on a number of grounds. First, there is as yet little evidence of impending uprisings by ill-equipped black majorities against white governments with sophisticated weapons systems. Second, and more important, western powers are still in the process of retrenching from overseas commitments and are acquiring a detached view of their responsibility in decolonization. And third, direct responses by western powers are much more likely to be guided by shrewd calculations of significant or vital national interest; these do not appear to include becoming involved in a bitter race war in far off lands. Past experience regarding the cold war is, in this context, not a useful guide.

On the liberation movements' prospects for success in replacing their target governments without external assistance, in the face of continued resistance by the incumbent regimes, observers are generally pessimistic, even when their

sympathies lie with the insurgents.   A partial listing of the obstacles the insurgents face will illustrate the point.   They include (1) initial lack of experience, training, and clear estimate of enemy capabilities, (2) tensions over
the relative usefulness of military operations and political control, (3) ideological disputes among leadership groups, (4) defections by both leaders and guer-
rilla groups, resulting in bitter denunciations and recriminations, (5) difficulties
in securing widespread public support, (6) failures of tactical alliances, (7) problems in maintaining a given movement's autonomy and ensuing internecine
fights and armed clashes with rival groups in the same territory, (8) competition
for external aid and recognition, (9) the overall effectiveness of incumbent
governments, and (10) the many frustrations arising out of enormous costs and
sacrifices for goals receding farther into the future.   Finally, there are the
cumulative consequences of the exile condition to which some attention is now
being paid.   That condition has led to innumerable problems, such as the dis-
couraging of free speech and criticism, the use of strongarm tactics against
internal and external opponents, or racial, psychological, ideological, religious, personal, and structural irritants which become magnified in exile.

Most Africa scholars agree that these liberation movements by themselves have
little chance for achieving their objectives in the immediate future.   This
holds true of observers who emphasize shortcomings of doctrine, psychological
variables, inefficient organization, or inability (with the exception of Guinea-
Bissau) to mobilize significant public support.   Sheridan Johns, in reviewing
current prognostications concerning South Africa, suggests a generalization
which may apply to most.   He finds "virtually unanimous agreement that early
efforts to mount armed struggle . . . were doomed to failure, and that future
efforts have little chance of success in the short, if not in the long, run"
(Johns, "Obstacles," p. 294).

Theories of guerilla warfare should ideally encompass both military (short-run)
and political (long-run) considerations.   But beyond this truism there is much
room for disagreement about the relative priority assigned to each component,
and the leaders of African liberation movements have disagreed.

One school emphasizes conventional Marxist-Leninist doctrine, according to
which a revolutionary situation must precede the actual revolution, a kind of
"politics before armed struggle" view.   Proponents of this school recommend
preparatory activities by revolutionary vanguards to arouse people's conscious-
ness of their plight and their relative deprivation to persuade them that eventual revolution is the only way out of their predicament.   The need now is
for building cadres and revolutionary structures at home, against the day when
armed struggle becomes an effective possibility.   This theory holds also that
external aid is of the greatest consequence, an idea actively espoused by
Soviet leaders in their policy toward African liberation movements.

Another school, that favored by the People's Republic of China, may be called
one of "armed struggle before politics."   It holds that a premium be placed on
action, now.   Guerillas must show through example, with only negligible sup-

port by the bulk of the population if necessary, that military victories can be won through tactics and through the slow acquisition of forward bases of operation in the target areas. Underlying assumptions include a belief that existing authority is not immune and that violence itself is a cleansing, catalytic reagent. Thus, guerilla violence is expected to transform those who participate, and indirectly those who observe and approve, from hesitant bystanders to heroic participants. The phenomenon is expected to spread in concentric circles and eventually affect the entire population. Repressive action by incumbent governments is thought to reinforce and quicken the process, and, since historical inevitability is on the insurgents' side, short-term sacrifices must be borne with fortitude. The Castro-Debray school, considerably reinforced by the writings of Frantz Fanon, tends to endow the liberation struggle with some mystical qualities. It suggests instant revolutions propitiating the catalysts of violence and erupting into full-fledged insurrections and rapid final victories.

Guerilla leaders have not embraced these theories wholesale, although many believe parts of them. Imported theories of guerilla warfare are also no guarantees of success. Nonetheless, they can have inspirational value and hence should not be lightly dismissed. The Chinese model, for instance, is a doctrine tailormade for the underdog, and it is capable of instilling optimism in the face of an adverse struggle against vastly superior forces. That model emphasizes not only that time is on the side of the just cause, but also that men are infinitely more important than weapons or technologically superior enemy forces; that but a few dedicated men are needed for an effective revolutionary nucleus; and that temporary failures teach guerillas the bitter lessons needed for greater effectiveness. As one observer explains, the Chinese model, "a complex . . . doctrine, if fully implemented is a coherent and practical body of belief likely to serve an armed band better than slogans or mere enthusiasm" (Larkin, CHINA, p. 124).

Elements from these schools of thought were adapted in an eclectic fashion over time to African conditions. The specifically African theoretical underpinnings of guerilla struggle which emerge from a reading of their leaders' public pronouncements and published writings are meager. "African theories of guerilla warfare are truncated, disjointed, unrefined, eclectic, nebulous, and situationally specific . . . [and] have yet to be written," wrote Grundy (GUERILLA, p. 165). Since spectacular success in the field is lacking, theoretical guidance for African liberation movements has become pagmatic. In the early 1960s some theories predicted results almost overnight. When initial attempts to use urban centers as theaters of guerilla operations backfired, early theories and strategies were modified. "The level of comprehension of and dedication to the time variable does not appear to be as far advanced in Africa as in Asia," Grundy noted (GUERILLA, p. 163).

More recent appraisals favor the first school, which emphasizes planning and preparation. It may be that as Africans slowly recognize that foreign assistance has limited effectiveness, they are reorienting their thinking toward greater self-reliance. Recently African liberation movements have paid greater attention to the nature of the conflict and the need for operating among the rural masses rather than in urban areas. Realization of the need for rural support seems related not so much to theoretical speculation, nor to the obvious fact that more than 90 percent of the people are farmers, but seems rather the result of shrewd calculation and of improved understanding of the political process on a national scale in Africa. Leadership groups are drawn mostly from urban areas, and they probably understand that successful military and political struggles require rural support.

One major theme found among African guerilla groups has been that of the national, as opposed to the regional or provincial, struggle. How much this theoretical emphasis on the national liberation struggle can bridge these states' immense problems of multidimensional fragmentation remains to be seen. With one exception African liberation movements are not yet, strictly speaking, national movements. They are national in intent, in that they plan to liberate and subsequently govern the territory which they consider the nation. But they are less than national in scope, since their support is drawn chiefly from one or two ethnic groups rather than a full representation of the future nation and since a given liberation movement's activities take place in only one territorial segment of the future nation. In many ways their experience approximates the history of political movements and parties elsewhere in Africa. Support and activities are circumscribed by divisions in social structure and space, and the overall struggle also involves infighting and jockeying for position among contending groups.

Studies of relations between liberation movements and incumbent governments, and the enormous imbalance of military forces and capabilities, suggest that the struggle will become a long confrontation, slowly but somehow inexorably leading to eventual majority rule. Initial estimates have been readjusted and timetables lengthened accordingly from a few years to a few decades. Few observers believe that the personnel and attitudes of governments will change, save as part of fanciful speculation. Grundy suggested, speculatively, that junior officers in Lisbon force the government to resign in 1990 (GUERILLA, p. 187).

He could not forsee that this would happen in April 1974. The event raises fresh hopes that incumbent elites may also adapt to change elsewhere in southern Africa, whether or not this is related to the strains of continued struggle. The Portuguese coup d'etat paved the way for transforming the conflict from a guerilla struggle to one about the nature of the forthcoming political settlement and the duration of the transition period. The ability of the black African groups in these territories to compose their differences is a function of many interrelated factors. These include their relative degree of control over population and territory, their ability to provide essential public services, Portuguese policies of favoritism or impartiality, the strength and direction of traditional ethnic animosities, the political acumen of top leaders, the policies adopted by contiguous and other African states, the efforts of the OAU, and the interest shown by extra-African national, transnational, and international groups and organizations. Events in the former Portuguese territories will therefore be watched very carefully.

There are major differences between the Portuguese areas and Rhodesia and South Africa. From Lisbon, African territories are essentially extra-continental, foreign areas from which European settlers could return home to the colonial power which controlled them. For whites in South Africa and Rhodesia, who think of themselves only as Africans, there is no colonial mother country of which to return, and ceding the territory to black Africans would be like abandoning one's homeland. The Portuguese case therefore may not be a model for the rest of southern Africa. But the developments may have some implications for change, or avoidance of change. Portuguese governments after April 1974 were marked by disunity, naivete, and confusion, and the fragmentation of the emerging Portuguese political system contributed to the country's political and military weakness in dealing with African rebel groups. The initial attempt by the Portuguese to bring about change misfired because it was inspired by an outdated, imperial view. Liberation movements have been reluctant to share political power, among themselves and with other aspiring structures, and they have been guided by their strength inside a given territory. Cooperation between Lisbon and the rebels replaced armed conflict. Portugal retained considerable influence over the transition process and the laying of foundations for future political and economic structures. The Portuguese and the rebels cooperated also in the sensitive area of containment of diehards. Moreover, both Portugal and rebel groups sought and secured cooperation from independent African states in easing the transition period.

Beyond what decolonization the Portuguese experience produces, the events themselves will have considerable impact on the enduring recalcitrant regimes. Aside from the obvious psychological impact of the coup, the most important change is geographic. The boundaries of the struggle may now shift southward, giving rebels direct access to two-thirds of Rhodesia's frontiers and to South Africa and Swaziland in the east as well as South West Africa in the west. Rhodesia is far more vulnerable than South Africa, and strategies may concentrate on that area. Since a major intervention in Rhodesia by South Africa is unlikely, the white population in Rhodesia may choose an interim political settlement providing for majority participation in government and a schedule for eventual majority rule rather than continued, costly guerilla warfare and increasing international pressures.

The most promising avenue to decolonization in southern Africa is that of altering the values and commitments of the incumbent government, political elites, and economic and social leaders. The lesson for South Africa from the Portuguese events is that change is least expensive when it comes from within. South Africa's leaders should be able to develop a formula for sharing, instead of turning over, power and for removing the political obstacles to South African cooperation with the rest of Africa.

B. LIBERATION MOVEMENTS

199   Bell, J. Bowyer. THE MYTH OF THE GUERILLA: REVOLUTIONARY
         THEORY AND MALPRACTICE. New York: Knopf, 1971. 268 p. Bibliography, index.

A study of why revolutionary guerillas persevere against enormous odds and suffer formidable sacrifice without any assurance
of success. Bell suggests that they are sustained by a myth
transcending not only repeated failure and vastly superior enemy
resources, but also the likelihood of eventual defeat. Whatever the errors committed or illusions entertained, these are
compensated for by an unquestioning faith linked to frustration
and despair: it is better to live for an ideal capable of sus-
taining the dignity of independent decisions and a belief in
eventually remaking man than to endure a seamless web of humiliation. Bell suggests that such a myth, whose attributes he
discusses at some length, plus the solace of mere action it le-
gitimizes, may be independent from the justice of a cause.
Some revolutionary guerilla activity may thus be a messianic
psychological-religious phenomenon far removed from conventional warfare or even guerilla struggle.

200 Cabral, Amilcar. RETURN TO THE SOURCE: SELECTED SPEECHES OF
AMILCAR CABRAL. New York: Monthly Review, 1974. 106 p. Reading list, illustrations.

A collection of Cabral's major addresses delivered in the United
States, to which is appended a list of writings by and about
the Guinean leader.

201 _____. REVOLUTION IN GUINEA: SELECTED TEXTS. Translated by
Richard Handyside. New York and London: Monthly Review, 1970.
174 p. Appendix.

A selection of essays by an outstanding African leader, on subjects ranging from the social structure of the country (for which
he eventually gave his life) to advice on strategy and tactics,
the role of the United Nations, and the cause of liberation.

202 Chaliand, Gerard. ARMED STRUGGLE IN AFRICA: WITH THE GUE-
RILLAS IN 'PORTUGUESE' GUINEA. Translated by David Rattray and
Robert Leonhardt. New York: Monthly Review, 1969. 125 p. Ap-
pendices, bibliography.

An account of the author's 1966 visit to Guinea in liberated
areas, preceded by brief descriptive comments on the country
and followed by speculation about guerilla fighters. Criticisms
of guerilla groups elsewhere in Africa dwell on their lack of
understanding for realities, dedication, training, their absence
from the target areas, and excessive dependence on external
help. Based on the Guinean experience, Chaliand suggests
that one good way to succeed is to adopt a two-phase strategy:
one of political implantation, involving agitation and propaganda,
enlistment of the most receptive peasant groups, training of
cadres, and a growing revolutionary structure, and another of

military implantation, to demonstrate martial abilities under
close political control, and to create a position of strength for
political negotiations with the enemy.

203   Davidson, Basil. THE LIBERATION OF GUINEA: ASPECTS OF AN
AFRICAN REVOLUTION. Baltimore: Penguin, 1969. 160 p. Paperback.

An engrossing, highly favorable, personal account of the liberation struggle, based on a 1967 visit and extensive research.
The book is mainly historical, but also focuses on questions of
principles and organization, objectives, and nature of the
struggle.

204   Day, John. INTERNATIONAL NATIONALISM: THE EXTRA-TERRITORIAL
RELATIONS OF SOUTHERN RHODESIAN AFRICAN NATIONALISTS.
London: Routledge and Kegan Paul; New York: Humanities Press, 1967.
136 p. Appendix.

An examination of the development of the foreign links fash-
ioned by the black African nationalists of southern Rhodesia in
Britain, with international organizations, and in Central Africa,
as well as the difficulties inherent in operating from abroad.
In evaluating the usefulness of such foreign activities, the study
concludes that the revolution can be successful only if supported
by the people at home.

205   Gibson, Richard. AFRICAN LIBERATION MOVEMENTS: CONTEMPO-
RARY STRUGGLES AGAINST WHITE MINORITY RULE. New York:
Oxford University Press, 1972. 328 p. Tables, paperback.

A passionate review of African movements for liberation from
colonial and white-dominated rule in South Africa, South West
Africa, Rhodesia, the Portuguese territories of Angola, Mozambique, Guinea, and Sao Tome e Principe; the French Territory
of the Afar and Issa; the Comoros; and the Canary Islands.
This basic background book does not hesitate to find fault with
some of the liberation movements' behaviors. The writer believes that revolutionary violence alone can bring about basic
change.

206   Gross, Ernest A. "The Coalescing Problem of Southern Africa." FOR-
EIGN AFFAIRS 46 (July 1968): 743-57.

A review of the situation in southern Africa and a criticism of
the U.S. government for cynical inconsistencies between actual
policy and commitment to the United Nations charter.

207   Grundy, Kenneth W. CONFRONTATION AND ACCOMMODATION IN
SOUTHERN AFRICA: THE LIMITS OF INDEPENDENCE. Berkeley and

Los Angeles: University of California Press, for the Center on International Race Relations, University of Denver, 1973. 323 p. Maps, tables, figures, bibliography.

A major study of international relations among the political units of southern Africa, focusing on such interaction elements as ideology and race, economics, politics, and violence. The author gives attention to the efforts of some moderate African leaders who are willing to experiment with a combination of pragmatism and reason and to South African efforts to break out of its isolation. The approach is informed by systems analysis as well as by concepts of foreign policy behavior. The state of relations in the southern African subsystem is fluid and hence susceptible to change, in part because that system is removed from direct great power confrontation, and in part because state behavior varies on different issues. The long-term prospect is unstable, but the short-term favors the white-controlled regimes.

208 ____. GUERILLA STRUGGLE IN AFRICA: AN ANALYSIS AND PRE-VIEW. New York: Grossman, 1971. 188 p. Appendices, paperback.

An imaginative and well-grounded thinkpiece. After an excursion into causes of violence in a discussion centered on "relative deprivation," and after a short treatment of African notions of violence, there is a somewhat convoluted treatment of doctrine. A typology of guerilla movements includes those fighting against incumbent independent African governments. Grundy is pessimistic about the ability of liberation movements to succeed without significant external help. Addressing the longer range, he presents a utopian scenario of majority rule—including a military takeover in Portugal. A major assumption is that if public opinion in western countries were only informed, it would respond favorably and pressure western governments into action.

209 Johns, Sheridan. "Obstacles to Guerilla Warfare—A South African Case Study." JOURNAL OF MODERN AFRICAN STUDIES 11 (June 1973): 267-303.

An outline of the development of the two black nationalist movements, from initial mass protests to select violence and repression. This article also considers the constraints of operating from abroad, doctrinal and tactical changes, and emphasis on black nationalism. The major problem is the mobilization of support inside South Africa and, the author suggests, the abandoning of a deep-rooted gradualist approach.

210 Marcum, John. THE ANGOLAN REVOLUTION. Vol. I: THE ANATOMY OF AN EXPLOSION (1950-1962). Cambridge: Massachusetts Institute of Technology, 1969. 319 p. Appendices, illustrations.

A classic, historical study of the rise of nationalism, rebellion,

and revolution in Angola, informed by meticulous research and
strong sympathies.

211   Mondlane, Eduardo. THE STRUGGLE FOR MOZAMBIQUE. Baltimore:
       Penguin, 1969. 222 p. Illustrations, paperback.

       A review, written by the former leader of an important gue-
       rilla movement in Mozambique (assassinated in 1969), of salient
       aspects of Portuguese colonialism and of the drive for indepen-
       dence.

212   Stokke, Olav, and Widstrand, Carl, eds. SOUTHERN AFRICA: THE
       UN--OAU CONFERENCE, OSLO 9--14 APRIL 1974. Uppsala, Sweden:
       Scandinavian Institute of African Studies, 1973. Vol. I: PROGRAMME
       OF ACTION AND CONFERENCE PROCEEDINGS. 263 p. Appendix,
       paperback. Vol. II: PAPER AND DOCUMENTS. 340 p. Appendix,
       paperback.

       A testimonial to growing Scandinavian interest in and support
       for African liberation movements in southern Africa. These
       two collections of documents highlight the continued interna-
       tionalization of the issue. The first volume includes the Oslo
       Conference recommendations, a resume of the plenary session,
       and edited discussions. The second volume presents background
       papers on the liberation struggle in the areas affected and a
       survey of support from international organizations and individual
       governments and groups. Of particular interest are differences
       in perceptions by those directly affected, those most able to
       contribute, and those in the process of increasing their aware-
       ness.

213   Venter, Al J. PORTUGAL'S WAR IN GUINEA-BISSAU. Pasadena:
       California Institute of Technology, Munger Africana Library Notes, no.
       19, April 1973. 202 p. Illustrations, paperback.

       An excellent account of the war, written by a journalist. It
       is one of the few available in this country which is on balance
       favorable to the Portuguese, although it is fair and expresses
       admiration for the rebels. The fifteen chapters describe combat
       experience, involvements of black Africans in fighting on both
       sides, as well as people and land. Since the Portuguese were
       fighting because of a mixture of motives and by western stan-
       dards were not enormously efficient, success for their cause
       depended in a large part on the personal qualities of their
       commander, General Antonio de Spinola, who was later re-
       moved and became the Portuguese armed forces titular chief
       after their revolt in Portugal. Because of the complexity of
       conditions and motives on both sides, this book does not fit
       into the mold of either revolutionary purity or Portuguese de-
       fense of western civilization. Success in war is partly a matter
       of chance.

214 _____. THE TERROR FIGHTERS: A PROFILE OF GUERILLA WARFARE IN SOUTHERN AFRICA. Cape Town: Purnell, 1969. 152 p. Illustration.

A guided tour with the Portuguese forces--black and white-- in Angola. The book is filled with highly personalized vignettes, but it conveys the deadlines, sacrifice, ignorance, and pathos of insurgency and repression.

Chapter 6
REFERENCE WORKS

A. GENERAL BIBLIOGRAPHIES

A CURRENI BIBLIOGRAPHY ON AFRICAN AFFAIRS. Westport, Conn.: Greenwood Periodicals Co. for the African Bibliographic Center, Washington, D.C. 1962--. Bimonthly, then monthly from 1968 to 1970, then bimonthly, then quarterly since 1974.

> A basic research tool, organized in four sections. Section 1 contains brief articles, occasionally on international relations topics. Section 2 reviews books individually or on a comparative basis, the subject depending upon publication and editorial selection. Some of the reviews concern international relations. Section 3, the largest, is devoted to references. It is divided into two subsections. The first is general and frequently includes listings on reference materials, on bibliographies and bibliographic essays, as well as on foreign aid, foreign economic relations, foreign investments, military affairs, the Organization of African Unity, and on African relations with other countries. The second subsection is devoted to regions (geographic and by colonial power), with separate entries about individual states. Section 4 is an author index, with cross-references to section 3. The entries include sources published mostly in Africa, the United States, Europe, and Canada; many are briefly annotated.

Dale, Doris Cruger. "Suggested Readings on Southern Africa." In SOUTHERN AFRICA IN PERSPECTIVE: ESSAYS IN REGIONAL POLITICS, edited by Christian P. Potholm and Richard Dale, pp. 398–406. New York: Free Press; London: Collier-Macmillan, 1972.

> An extensive, though selective, listing of books, documents, and articles on the topic.

Duignan, Peter, ed., and Conover, Helen, comp. GUIDE TO AFRICAN RESEARCH AND REFERENCE WORKS. Hoover Institution Bibliographical Series: XLVI. Stanford: Hoover Institution Press, 1970. 941 p. Index, pp. 945–1102.

A thorough and fundamental reference work, divided into four parts. Part 1 is a general guide and treats research centers, institutions, and records; European, North American, and African libraries and archives; and publishers and bookdealers. Part 2 lists bibliographies of bibliographies, lists of serials and acquisitions, official publications, dissertations, and atlases and maps. Part 3 is a subject guide which lists not only general reference works but also eighteen subjects from "Arts and Letters" to "Traditional Religion and Thought." Part 4 divides the subject by area, including former colonial power, region, and individual country. Parts 1 and 4 have brief introductions. The volume has 3,126 entries.

INTERNATIONAL AFRICAN BIBLIOGRAPHY. London: International African Institute, 1973--. Quarterly.

A continuation of the bibliography published in the quarterly AFRICA, the journal of the International African Institute, between 1929 and 1972. Since 1973 it has been published by the Library of the School of Oriental and African Studies, University of London. Sections 6 "Economics and Development," and 7, "Political Science," are most likely to list entries of interest to students of international relations and foreign policy. It contains an annual author index.

Jumba-Masagazi, A.H.D., comp. AFRICAN SOCIALISM: A BIBLIOGRAPHY. Nairobi: The East African Academy, 1970. 68 p. Biographic notes, paperback.

A sound research tool for anyone interested in understanding or pursuing the topic. The bibliography, covering the years between 1948 and 1970, is preceded by a discussion of topics including the concept, background, and different views on African socialism and is complemented by a list of serials and a list of useful addresses on four continents.

Minogue, Martin, and Molloy, Judith, eds. AFRICAN AIMS AND ATTITUDES: SELECTED DOCUMENTS. London: Cambridge University Press, 1974. 376 p. Biographies, bibliography, paperback.

Brief but cogent excerpts from the writings of some thirty-five African leaders, as well as key documents and manifestoes. Part 1, on colonialism and decolonization, has thirteen entries. Part 2 is on nation-building and includes a number of documents related to international affairs. Part 3, on pan-Africanism, is divided into sections on institutions, leaders, and culture. Part 4 presents materials on international organizations, on southern Africa, and on neocolonialism. Part 5 includes statements by African military leaders in political office (and one by Nkrumah, one of their opponents).

Mytelka, Lynn K. "A Genealogy of Francophone West and Equatorial African Regional Organizations." JOURNAL OF MODERN AFRICAN STUDIES 12 (June 1974): 297-320.

The first part of this essay analyzes integration efforts, focusing on the following factors: the lack of "a dynamic 'core area,'" nationalism, and the role of external actors as partial factors. The essay also explores the direction of these former French-sponsored associations, and the consequences for integration of initiatives taken by African leaders. The second part (pp. 310-20) is a bibliography divided into twelve sections; this includes general bibliographies and other sources, as well as references on eight associations and one miscellaneous integration effort.

* Paden, John N., and Soja, Edward W., eds. THE AFRICAN EXPERIENCE, VOLUME IIIA: BIBLIOGRAPHY. Evanston, Ill.: Northwestern University Press, 1970. 1103 p.

A major work by any standards. It contains more than 4,000 references. Several considerations guided the editors. First, the volume is intended in part as a companion to two other works in this series, one of essays and another a syllabus intended for class use. Second, the editors have included works in French, on the grounds that more than one-half of Africa's states use that language as their official and scholarly tongue. Third, they point out that, because of the lag between research priorities and the publication of the results of research, this volume probably reflects research priorities of the five-year period preceding it.

The volume is divided into three sections. Section 1 follows the topical outline of the syllabus. Distinctions between national and international affairs are often arbitrary. Such topics as African reactions to colonialism, the behavior of elites, or notions of nationalism, for instance, are all relevant to international relations. Nonetheless, part 5 of section 1 is devoted to twenty-one topics under the specific heading of "Africa and the Modern World." These contain references to Africa and [country or region], southern Africa, relations with black Americans, inter-African relations, as well as such modern developments as in architecture, music, and social thought. There is also an epilog treating problems of social scientists and Africa, including attention to concepts in the social sciences, the conduct of research in Africa, and research frontiers.

Since the authors believe that in African studies, "attempts at generalization are premature" (p. xv), they have included case-study references. This comprises section 2, divided into forty-two independent states, and four areas which continue to experience

___

* Items thus marked are recommended for a library list.

colonial rule. Rhodesia and South West Africa are classified as
nonindependent, whereas South Africa is regarded as independent.
All entries are cross-referenced when they appear more than once
in either section. The authors point out that the quality of the
references varies considerably because little systematic literature
is available for most African states. In this section on country
references, part 5 is again devoted to "Africa and the Modern
World," in turn separated into International Relations and Literature and Intellectual Thought; part 6 consists of entries on "General Materials and on Bibliographies." Finally, the third section
is devoted to an author index, each entry being cross-referenced
to the listings in the first two sections.

Pearson, J.D., and Jones, Ruth, eds. THE BIBLIOGRAPHY OF AFRICA:
PROCEEDINGS AND PAPERS OF THE INTERNATIONAL CONFERENCE ON
AFRICAN BIBLIOGRAPHY, NAIROBI, 4-8 DECEMBER 1967. New York:
International African Institute, 1970. 238 p. Appendices.

A collection of twenty-five papers which discuss (1) individual
and common problems in four English-speaking and four French-
speaking African states, in east Africa, the Library of Congress,
the African Bibliographic Center in Washington, D.C., and at
Syracuse University; (2) holdings about African writers, languages,
emphemera, and questions of control, discography, and microfilm;
(3) recommendations for improving African holdings; (4) and bibliographic services available in fourteen African states, nine European countries, and the United States. The essays are preceded
by a chapter on the scope of the field as discussed at the conference which was sponsored by the International African Institute.

Smaldone, Joseph P., comp. "African Liberation Movements: An Interim
Bibliography." AFRICAN STUDIES NEWSLETTER (Published by the African
Studies Association) 7 (June 1974): 17.

This collection is divided into five parts: bibliographies (14 entries); books, theses, and reports (74 entries); articles, chapters,
and papers (189 entries); pamphlets (52 entries); and information
issued by African liberation movements (132 entries). Parts 2,
3, and 4 are in turn divided into a general section and one each
on Angola, Guinea-Bissau, Mozambique, Namibia, and Zimbabwe.
Part 5, in addition to the above, includes references on Botswana, the Cameroons, the Comoro Islands, Ethiopia, Ghana,
Lesotho, South Africa, Swaziland, Zanzibar, and Portuguese Africa. It was compiled by Susan K. Rishworth on the basis of
holdings at the Library of Congress.

SUB-SAHARAN AFRICA: A GUIDE TO SERIALS. Compiled by African Section, Reference Department, General Reference and Bibliography Division,
Library of Congress. Washington, D.C.: 1970. 409 p.

Most of this volume consists of alphabetical listings of serials (4,670 entries), followed by a subject index and an index of relevant organizations.

UNITED STATES AND CANADIAN PUBLICATIONS AND THESES ON AFRICA. Stanford, Calif.: Hoover Institution on War, Revolution, and Peace, 1962--. Annual. (The first volume was published by the African Section of the Library of Congress, and subsequent volumes by the Hoover Institution.)

After a brief section which lists the thirty to forty bibliographic references from which the information is drawn, the volumes are divided into two major parts; the volume covering the year 1966 (published in 1969) is a compilation of all books, pamphlets, and articles published in the United States and Canada. Information on doctoral theses completed on Africa in these two countries was added in 1965. The first part is arranged by topics and includes a section on international relations and one on pan-Africanism. The second part of the 1966 volume lists entries by individual country and by regions. The volume also includes an author, subject, and geographic index.

B. BIBLIOGRAPHIC ESSAYS

Dale, Richard. "Southern Africa: Research Frontiers in Political Science." In SOUTHERN AFRICA IN PERSPECTIVE: ESSAYS IN REGIONAL POLITICS, edited by Christian P. Potholm and Richard Dale, pp. 1-15. New York: Free Press; London: Collier-Macmillan, 1972.

This essay first reviews problems and status of data collection and storage, data retrieval, and institutionally sponsored research and publication on southern Africa, in Africa, Europe, and the United States. The second part addresses problems concerning further research. International affairs are discussed in systemic terms. It suggests the need for research on such aspects of the system of southern Africa as the relative strength of centripetal and centrifugal trends; surveys of elite attitudes in the component units; voting behavior in international organizations; foreign policy studies which cover relations within the system and with external agencies; the growth of nationalism; unconventional warfare; and the role of armed forces, police, and paramilitary structures. The author recognizes the practical obstacles confronting such research, such as censorship, and the moral dilemma involved in protecting informants and in the professional commitment to disclosure of sources.

Gardinier, David. "French Colonial Rule in Africa: A Bibliographical Essay." In FRANCE AND BRITAIN IN AFRICA: IMPERIAL RIVALRY AND COLONIAL RULE, edited by Prosser Gifford and Wm. Roger Louis, pp. 787-950. New Haven, Conn.: Yale University Press, 1971.

A detailed analytical survey of source materials. The section on

black Africa and Madagascar is divided by chronology and also
by topics such as political, economic, social, and constitutional
aspects of pre-independence antecedents of these states' international affairs. The essay is complemented by an analysis of various sources and by a bibliography.

Glickman, Harvey. "Political Science." In THE AFRICAN WORLD: A
SURVEY OF SOCIAL RESEARCH, edited by Robert A. Lystad, pp. 131-65.
New York: Praeger, 1965.

An international relations survey on the work done in this area.
Like other social scientists, these specialists have found that conceptual notions derived from earlier study of western states cannot
always explain what is occurring in Africa. Some students concentrated on political, economic, and cultural dimensions of pan-
Africanism, but the significance of this line of inquiry is not clear.
The author notes also that a few students concerned with the role
of Africa in the world have emphasized such questions as the cold
war, nonalignment, Communist penetration, relations with a few
small powers like Egypt and Israel, security and defense ties, and
the development of cultural ties, particularly with former metropolitan countries. Glickman suggests that the new ties developed
by independent African states are changing the international system, and sees the "development of a pattern of 'permanent,'
negotiated intervention by some states in the affairs of other states"
(p. 160). This development is precarious in view of growing opposition to what is perceived as neocolonial political and economic
exploitation, whatever the precise content of these terms.

* Paden, John N., and Soja, Edward W., eds. THE AFRICAN EXPERIENCE.
Vol. IIIB: GUIDE TO RESOURCES. Evanston, Ill.: Northwestern University
Press, 1970. 139 p.

This volume contains essays, with some complementary tables and
charts, on six topics. The first is a general, introductory essay
on reference sources. The second discusses African publishing
with a list of book publishers in black Africa. The third is on
African newspapers and journals and contains a selected listing of
African newspapers and of journals on Africa published in Africa,
Europe, Asia, and North America. The fourth is a specialized
treatment of African-language publications, concentrating on Hausa
and Swahili. The fifth chapter is on audiovisual materials about
Africa and contains a brief essay as well as a selected list of
available materials and distributors. The final chapter discusses
the application of computers to the compilation, storage, retrieval,
and printout of bibliographic materials about Africa.

C. HANDBOOKS

AFRICA 71. Edited and compiled by the editors of JEUNE AFRIQUE, Paris.
New York: Africana, 1971. 437 p. Maps, illustrations, tables.

A volume, third of a series of annuals, which combines relatively
brief descriptive and interpretive essays with up-to-date information and which is intended for the general reader as well as the
student. Part 1, "Africa at a Glance," includes essays on physical geography, weather, temperature, ethnic groups, vegetation,
population, and languages. Part 2, entitled "The Advanced
Countries and Africa," discusses relations between Africa and international organizations, the United States, Great Britain, France,
the USSR, and Japan. Part 3, "African Perspectives," presents essays on such topical subjects as the Nigerian civil war,
the east African community, hydroelectric development, and petroleum. The last part, the longest, reviews select recent developments in the continent, including Madagascar and Mauritius.
Each country has a section containing basic data apparently
modeled on French publications. Some of the data are four or
five years old and thus do not reflect the latest African government publications.

AFRICA SOUTH OF THE SAHARA, 1974. London: Europa Publications, 1974.
xxiv, 1115 p. Maps, tables.

A major work, divided into four parts, which is fourth in a series
of annuals. Part 1 includes ten general articles on background
information, of which four treat economic problems, two political
questions, and one each historical, linguistic, educational, and
religious topics. Part 2 is devoted to international regional organizations, both global and African, which have an interest in
Africa. The materials on these organizations are concise and
descriptive and contain information not easily found elsewhere,
including a list of regional organizations such as the International
Association for the Development of Libraries in Africa. Information on all international organizations includes lists of members,
organizational features, major activities, and publications issued.

Part 3 consists of country surveys of forty-eight political entities
on the mainland and offshore, politically dependent and independent (including Rhodesia and the Republic of South Africa which
many such sources exclude). The country sections are divided
into political, social, economic, and other categories. Essays
which complement tables and other compilations of data are written by well known students in their field, at times more than one
for each country; most are British, but some are African, French,
and American. Data are frequently more current than those of the
United Nations. The information tends to be complete and lists
diplomatic missions in or accredited to African states, although
unfortunately not the African states' own missions abroad. Each

country's survey ends with a small bibliography relying chiefly on British sources.

Many of the essays seem to lean toward the radical rather than moderate African persuasion, though writers are careful to lead through inference rather than flat statements and the approach used is more descriptive than analytical. Part 4, entitled "Other Reference Material," includes a Who's Who of present African personalities in Africa or in exile (some of the dead are not mentioned); data on various measures; a presentation on agricultural and mineral primary commodities; a list of institutions in thirty-six countries engaged in research on Africa; and a select bibliography of serials on Africa which is slightly outdated since it includes publications that expired a few years earlier.

Brownlee, Ian, ed. BASIC DOCUMENTS ON AFRICAN AFFAIRS. Oxford: Clarendon Press, 1971. 525 p. Appendices.

A useful background examination of major African international relations developments, although these must be supplemented. The volume is divided into six parts: the first concerns African international organizations; the second presents materials mostly on economic affairs; the third reproduces the 1965 Declaration on the Denuclearization of Africa by the UN General Assembly; the fourth is concerned with territorial issues; the fifth deals with self-determination in southern Africa; the sixth is about relations with extra-African states; and the seventh is concerned with events in the former Belgian Congo (now Zaire). The three appendices present materials on southern Africa, including the Lusaka Manifesto, the Stanleyville paratroop drop, and the Simonston agreement between Britain and South Africa regarding the use of the South African naval base.

Daggs, Elisa. ALL AFRICA: ALL ITS POLITICAL ENTITIES OF INDEPENDENCE OR OTHER STATUS. New York: Hastings House, 1970. 807 p. Maps, tables, appendix, index, illustrations.

A volume intended for the general reader, but which will be useful for more serious students because of its completeness. An introductory essay provides human and nonhuman background until modern independence. The bulk of the book comprises descriptive essays about states and territories, organized into three parts. Part 1 covers thirty-three states which have achieved political independence since 1957, part 2 the states and territories not yet under black majority rule, and part 3 those nations independent prior to 1957. Part 4 discusses general trends such as new international alignments and internal disturbances in independent states.

DIRECTORY OF AFRICAN STUDIES IN THE UNITED STATES. Waltham, Mass.: Brandeis University, African Studies Association, Research Liaison Committee, 1972. 204 p. Paperback.

The fourth in an annual series. This volume lists 327 universities
and colleges offering at least one course on the African continent,
in a total of fifty-five subject areas. Included is an index of
institutions and one of faculty (individually and by discipline),
as well as a language index listing thirty-four African languages
taught, from Afrikaans to Zulu.

Kitchen, Helen, ed. A HANDBOOK OF AFRICAN AFFAIRS. New York:
Praeger, for the African-American Institute, 1964. 311 p. Maps, paperback.

An introductory volume consisting of sketches of basic data and
brief discussions on several topics. Part 1 has some basic information on fifty-eight territorial units on the continent. Part 2
comes in two sections about African armed forces. The first section presents some statistics on the armed forces of and in forty-
two political units and brief comments, whereas the second section
singles out the role played by French military assistance to African
states. Part 3 concerns the Organization of African Unity. The
first section discusses the achievements of the 1963 conference in
Addis Ababa at which time the organization was created, the
second section presents the resolutions adopted at that conference,
and the third reproduces the text of the Charter of the Organization of African Unity. Part 4 consists of four brief introductory
essays on African literature and poetry.

Legum, Colin, ed. AFRICA: A HANDBOOK. 2d ed. London: Blond,
1965. 522 p. Maps, illustrations, index.

A handbook containing basic information about fifty-three political
entities on the continent and offshore. These are divided into
overlapping categories of geographic regions (the former British
territories), colonial power (the former French, as well as the
Portuguese and Spanish, territories), except for Madagascar, French
Somaliland, and the former Belgian Congo, listed under East Africa, Northwest Africa, and Central Africa, respectively. Individual essays treat each of the former British territories grouped
by colonial power. The second part is devoted to descriptive
essays on art and literature, religions, culture, economics, and
"attitudes toward Africans" by Great Britain, France, the United
States, and the Soviet Union.

* _____ . AFRICA CONTEMPORARY RECORD: ANNUAL SURVEY AND
DOCUMENTS 1972-73. New York: Africana, 1973. 1160 p. Maps,
tables, index.

The fourth in an annual series, an indispensable reference work
for anyone interested in keeping abreast of what happens in Africa.
Part 1 contains seventeen essays on current issues, including Africa's relations with Western Europe, the Soviet Union, Romania,
the People's Republic of China, Japan, Canada, Israel, the Arab

states, as well as on the Organization of African Unity and the
Organisation Commune Africaine, Malgache, et Mauricienne.
Part 2 consists of reviews of major events in fifty-two states and
terrirories divided into north, east, southern, central, and west
Africa; these essays include the quaint--penalties for wearing
miniskirts or killing cats--but mostly focus on important internal
and external developments and relations. Part 3 presents an abun-
dance of documents divided into three categories. First, a section on international relations which emphasizes international organizations, liberation movements, relations with other parts of
the world, and particular crises such as the expulsion of Asians
from Uganda. The second section, entitled "Political Issues,"
singles out major developments in fourteen states. The third section is devoted to more general reviews of such issues as trade,
education, the press, and communications.

Morrison, Donald George, et al., eds. BLACK AFRICA: A COMPARATIVE
HANDBOOK. New York: Free Press; London: Collier-Macmillan, 1972.
483 p.

Part 1 presents data in 172 tables--on the same number of vari-
ables--and discussion on comparative profiles, divided into sections on (1) demography, ecology, and pluralism, (2) social and
economic development, (3) political development, (4) security systems and stability, (5) international linkages, and (6) urban and
ethnic patterns. Part 2 discusses and presents data on thirty-two
country profiles of independent African states excluding the Portuguese areas, Rhodesia, and South Africa. Part 3 contains discussions and data on a variety of methodological problems and
issues about cross-national research, including (1) organization
and theory, (2) limitations and use of cross-national data, (3) reliability of data, and (4) classification and analysis of ethnic units.
There are five appendices which treat data and the use of com-
puter programs, codebook samples, correlation matrix, population
estimates, and a data bank for national integration data on Africa.
A detailed listing of tables is provided on pp. xii-xxi. Given
the interdependence of data on individual nations and on relations
between nations, much of the information presented is useful to
students of international affairs. The section on International
Linkages is divided into segments on economic assistance, external trade, and international relations; the latter presents information on diplomatic missions, membership in international organizations, and international conflict.

D. WHO'S WHO

Dickie, John, and Rake, Alan. WHO'S WHO IN AFRICA: THE POLITICAL,
MILITARY, AND BUSINESS LEADERS OF AFRICA. London: Wheatsheaf
House, 1973. 602 p.

For each of forty-seven countries on the continent, a brief, terse, basic presentation of factual data and essential political dates, followed by biographies of prominent leaders.

Fung, Karen. "Index to 'Portraits' in West Africa, 1948-1966." AFRICAN STUDIES BULLETIN 9 (December 1966): 103-20.

Melady, Thomas Patrick. PROFILES OF AFRICAN LEADERS. New York: Macmillan; Galt, Ont.: Brett-Macmillan, 1961. 180 p. Index.

A pioneering effort which provides brief sketches in nine chapters on prominent African political leaders and one chapter on another five personalities.

Segal, Ronald. AFRICAN PROFILES. Baltimore: Penguin, 1962. 343 p. Index, paperback.

Portraits of sixty-four political personalities from the African continent, including nine from former French areas below the Sahara.

E. UNITED STATES GOVERNMENT DOCUMENTS

i. Department of State

To help coordinate social science research sponsored by the U.S. government, some twenty-five government agencies agreed in 1964 to establish an interdepartmental Foreign Affairs Research (FAR) Coordinating Group. The FAR Secretariat is located in the State Department's Office of External Research, which also provides the assistance needed by the group's various subcommittees. The subcommittees divide their tasks along regional (including Africa) and functional lines. The Office of External Research has served as a partial clearinghouse for listing information on private research undertaken with or without the benefit of government sponsorship. As part of this activity the office publishes two documents available by subscription. One is MONTHLY PAPERS AVAILABLE. Individuals may request copies of papers listed from the Office of External Research directly if they were produced under State Department auspices, and others by contacting the authors. The second publication, called FAR HORIZONS, is a quarterly newsletter listing research programs about foreign affairs.

In 1971 the National Security Council's Under Secretaries Committee established a Subcommittee on Foreign Affairs Research (USC/FAR) for the purpose of coordinating external research sponsored by the six member agencies; these are the Departments of State and Defense, the Agency for International Development, the Arms Control and Disarmament Agency, the United States Information Agency, and the National Security Council Staff.

Chaired by the State Department's Director of Intelligence and Research, the USC/FAR issued its third consolidated research plan in 1973, and its fourth in 1974. These plans cover estimates for expenditures on foreign affairs research for fiscal years 1974-75 and 1975-76 (the National Security Staff planned no expenditures during this period), summarize proposed activities, discuss research objectives, and present detailed information on estimates in tabular form, broken down into a variety of categories such as regional and functional emphases.

A brief summary of these two plans is useful in this context. First, some hope was expressed for increased research funding in fiscal year 1974-75, but estimates for the fourth plan were slightly lower than for the third. Second, two of the five agencies' plans for that period show a trend toward increase (the Agency for International Development with 75 percent of the total, and the State Department with a projected 6 percent of the total), whereas the share of others is declining. Third, most of the research is planned in national affairs, and only about 16 percent was earmarked for international affairs. The report does not distinguish clearly between national and international affairs in its discussion, so that the two occasionally overlap. And finally, although the African continent (including North Africa but excluding Egypt) stood out as the most popular region for total research funding, only slightly above one percent of the total five-agency allocation was described as international relations research.

The bulk of the interest in Africa apparent in the third plan report was generated by the Agency for International Development, which planned originally to set aside about one-third of its research funds for that region. But total interagency research funding for Africa dropped from about 30 percent to 3.4 percent in the fourth plan (fiscal year 1975-76). Of that latter percentage, about half was budgeted for military relations; the two largest single amounts were earmarked for the categories of "international ideologies and movements" and "military assistance and sales," thus reflecting an apparent emphasis on ideological and hardnosed economic and defense criteria. The other agencies planned to allocate less than 10 percent of their respective totals to Africa. In Africa the Agency for International Development's interest in Africa gave priority in the first plan to agriculture, demography, and social services, and in the third to national economic policies.

The State Department also publishes a number of documents and pamphlets on select aspects of American policy toward Africa and on research conducted on that part of the world. These can serve as background materials for initial familiarization as well as for building blocs for further research. Among the numerous documents published by the Department of State, those of particular interest for American foreign relations in Africa include the following:

AFRICAN PROGRAMS OF U.S. ORGANIZATIONS. Occasional lists of programs on Africa by nongovernmental organizations such as foundations and universities.

AMERICAN FOREIGN POLICY: CURRENT DOCUMENTS. An annual compilation of major published papers focusing on general policy and encompassing functional and geographic areas of policy.

BACKGROUND NOTES. Occasional issues on African states. These contain brief description of political and geographic background, lists of government officials, major resident U.S. government officials, and short reading lists.

CURRENT FOREIGN POLICY. Contains an African series, as part of occasional, brief reviews of American policy and pertinent select data, by country.

THE FOREIGN ASSISTANCE PROGRAM: ANNUAL REPORT TO THE CONGRESS. Annual pamphlets, issued from 1945 to 1971 covering the respective fiscal years. These documents provide specific and general information regarding American foreign assistance programs. The information is broken down into appropriation categories and specific programs for which assistance was disbursed. The report contains data for geographic regions and the individual countries therein, international organizations, and military assistance and sales to foreign countries. Tables and charts with data are also included. (This pamphlet was available from the Agency for International Development and its predecessor agencies until 1971; since that time no such document has been made available to the public.)

GEOGRAPHIC BULLETIN. Occasional brief surveys, such as AFRICA: PATTERNS OF SOVEREIGNTY, issued in 1968.

GIST. Occasional fact sheet on select problems of American foreign policy, issued by the Office of Plans and Management, Bureau of Public Affairs. It contains brief references to other State Department materials on the same subject. This series was formerly known as FOREIGN POLICY OUTLINES.

INTERNATIONAL ORGANIZATION SERIES. Occasional pamphlets with background information on the structure and politics of such organizations as the OAU and the UN, with brief comments on American foreign policy.

STATE DEPARTMENT BULLETIN. Weekly official record of speeches and government actions. Also included are lists of current documents.

UNITED STATES FOREIGN POLICY 1969-1970: A REPORT OF THE SECRETARY OF STATE. Department of State Publication 8575. General Foreign Policy Series 254. Revised March 1971. xx, 617 p. Maps, tables, charts, annex, paperback.

A six-part discussion follows an introductory statement by the Secretary of State. The first part is broken down into Europe, East Asia and Pacific, Near East and South Asia, the Americas, and

Africa. The second part focuses on international security policy including military policy and arms control. The third part is devoted to economic affairs and distinguishes between general, foreign economic policy and development assistance. The fourth part is called "International Organization and Law." The fifth is a discussion of the social and scientific dimension of American foreign relations. The final part reviews questions of foreign policy management and diplomacy and of resources for conducting American policy relations. The annex presents a variety of public documents and speeches by American officials, a list of treaties and agreements signed or ratified, and a list of major State Department officials.

UNITED STATES FOREIGN POLICY 1971: A REPORT OF THE SECRETARY OF STATE. Department of State Publication 8634. General Foreign Policy Series 260. Revised March 1972. xvii, 604 p. Maps, tables, charts, annex, paperback.

This report duplicates the one for 1969-70 and brings it up to date; breakdown and approximate size of parts are the same. (No such report has been issued since, although it apparently was planned as a series.)

ii. Department of Commerce

In 1968, the Africa Division of the Bureau of Commerce issued a supplement to the periodical International Commerce entitled "Africa: A Growth Market for U.S. Business." This publication contains (1) general descriptive articles about the African market, on American trade and investments, and on African industrial developments--three of the articles were written by government officials, including one on the Agency for International Development by a Deputy Assistant Secretary of State for African Affairs; (2) brief descriptions of continental and regional multilateral organizations devoted to African economic growth and development; (3) a section on investment laws in forty African states; (4) a section on African states' import restrictions and regulations, many of which were liberalized and otherwise altered in the intervening years; and (5) a number of appendices covering statistical materials relating to previous parts, and some indicators of political divisions in Africa as well as brief bibliographical references.

COMMERCE TODAY. 1969--. Biweekly. Formerly INTERNATIONAL COMMERCE (1962-69).

The second section is devoted to international trade and includes occasional articles on commercial relations with Africa; it also lists publications on international business.

OVERSEAS BUSINESS REPORT. Semiannual pamphlets entitled "Basic Data on the Economy of (individual African state)." These contain introductory data on important economic developments and opportunities, usually prepared by on-the-spot Foreign Service Officers, and distributed by the Bureau of International Commerce, as well as through the department's field offices across the United States.

TRADE OF THE UNITED STATES WITH AFRICA. Occasional reports on individual countries and commodities, usually covering the two years preceding the date of publication.

F. SERIALS

What follows is a selective listing of periodicals which devote space to topics of direct interest to students of international affairs and foreign policy in Africa. Occasional articles on this topic appear also in more general publications, particularly in journals on international affairs and political science. Newspaper coverage of Africa and American policy toward Africa in this country is spotty; most papers get such news from wire and other like services and often extract small amounts which they seem to use as fillers. Nationally read American newspapers which stand out for their attention to Africa include the NEW YORK TIMES, WASHINGTON POST, CHRISTIAN SCIENCE MONITOR, BALTIMORE SUN, and LOS ANGELES TIMES.

Additional serials titles on general and specific topics may be found in (1) the UNION LIST OF SERIALS IN LIBRARIES IN THE UNITED STATES AND CANADA. 3d ed. New York: H.W. Wilson, 1965, and (2) NEW SERIALS TITLES: A UNION LIST OF SERIALS COMMENCING PUBLICATION AFTER DECEMBER 31, 1949, Washington, D.C.: Library of Congress; New York: R.R. Bowker, 1973.

AFRICA CONFIDENTIAL. London: Research Publication Services, 1960--. Twenty-five times per year. Formerly AFRICA (1965-66).

> Short review of contemporary economic, political, and social developments, many with reference to international affairs. Sources frequently bring to light little known but significant information, with a good record for accuracy.

AFRICA DIGEST. London: African Publications Trust, 1952--. Bimonthly. In April 1975 this merged with AFRICA CURRENTS.

> Condensed reviews of publications on Africa, regarding both domestic and international developments. It includes in-depth country profiles and a book review section. AFRICA CURRENTS places emphasis on African perceptions of political, economic, and social events and trends.

AFRICAN FORUM. New York: American Society of African Culture, 1965-68. Quarterly.

Articles on contemporary developments, most written by scholars, statesmen, and other close observers. The journal contains feature articles and book reviews.

AFRICAN STUDIES REVIEW. Syracuse, N.Y.: African Studies Association, 1958--. Three times per year. Previously AFRICAN STUDIES BULLETIN (1958-70).

Reports on scholarship and research on a variety of topics on African studies, for use chiefly by professional students. It includes bibliographies and book reviews. Some attention to topics of international affairs and foreign policy.

*AFRICA REPORT. New York: African-American Institute, 1956--. Six issues per year. Previously AFRICA SPECIAL REPORT (1956-60).

Makes liberal use of on-the-spot sources, including reporters and scholars, to present topical articles on contemporary domestic and international events. It includes special reports, and a section on developments in individual countries and is one of the best widely available sources for keeping up with trends.

*AFRICA RESEARCH BULLETIN: ECONOMIC, FINANCIAL, AND TECHNICAL SERIES; POLITICAL, SOCIAL, AND CULTURAL SERIES. Exeter, Engl.: Africa Research, 1964--. Monthly.

Both series are essential research tools; they reproduce newspaper articles and radio broadcasts chiefly from African sources but also from European and other sources not otherwise readily found in the United States. The first series is divided into seven parts, including one each on domestic economic conditions, economic policies, production and marketing, planning, communications, inter-African cooperation, and developments with countries overseas. The political series includes sections on international political developments, political relations among nations, political developments in individual states and in nonindependent territories, as well as social and cultural events.

AFRICA TODAY. Denver, Colo.: Africa Today Associates, 1954--. Quarterly. It was formerly published by the American Committee on Africa (1954-66).

Articles, features, occasional editorials, book reviews, and listings of newly published materials on African political, social, economic, and literary developments. This is a journal of opinion, which tends to concentrate on southern Africa and racial problems, with increasingly greater emphasis on scholarly criteria.

AFRIQUE CONTEMPORAINE. Paris: 1961--. Bimonthly.

Brief but useful features, including special studies, texts and reviews of major documents, reviews of significant books and other writings about Africa, and biographical sketches of leading African personalities.

CANADIAN JOURNAL OF AFRICAN STUDIES. Ottawa: Canadian Association of African Studies, 1967--. Semiannual. Previously BULLETIN OF AFRICAN STUDIES IN CANADA.

Scholarly articles on a variety of topics, some occasionally relevant directly to international relations.

GENEVE-AFRIQUE/GENEVA-AFRICA. Geneva: Institut Africain de Geneve, 1962--. Quarterly.

Articles in both French and English on a variety of topics, special studies, bibliographies, bibliographic notes, and review essays. Some emphasis is given to topics of direct import to students of international affairs.

ISSUE: A QUARTERLY JOURNAL OF AFRICANIST OPINION. Waltham, Mass.: African Studies Association, 1971--.

A lively discourse, mostly on southern Africa and aspects of American policy toward Africa. It is intended for the lay reader rather than those association members who specialize in international affairs and foreign policy and is intended to convince rather than inform.

JEUNE AFRIQUE. Paris: 1960--. Weekly. Previously AFRIQUE ACTION (1960-61).

A review of political, economic, and social developments in domestic and foreign affairs. It includes book reviews, brief discussions of cultural affairs and of sports events. It is similar to TIME magazine in style and format.

JOURNAL OF MODERN AFRICAN STUDIES. Cambridge: Cambridge University Press, 1963--. Quarterly.

Articles on political, economic, and social developments as well as a section of specialized reviews of new trends entitled "Africana" and book reviews. Occasional articles are of direct concern to international affairs. It is intended more for the specialist than for the lay reader.

PRESENCE AFRICAINE. Paris: 1947--. Quarterly.

A review of cultural and literary developments, but with some emphasis on social and political thought, and thus of interest to students of international affairs.

WEST AFRICA. London: Cromwell House, 1905--. Weekly.

Surveys of former British Africa which emphasize economic and business news and developments. It includes also special reports on contemporary political and social events and book reviews.

G. LIBRARY LIST

The following entries are recommended as an abbreviated list of holdings for a small library for students, business executives, and government officials; the list provides basic and general substantive background and guidelines for further digging.

Reference works are those preceded by an asterisk in chapter 6, and they need not be repeated here. The following are a recommended list of basic books, their numbers corresponding to those in the bibliographic sections of the appropriate chapter: [11] Kamarck; [18] Nielsen; [41] Legum; [55] Zartman; [189] Legvold; [196] Larkin; [205] Gibson; and [207] Grundy.

AUTHOR INDEX

In addition to authors, this index includes all editors, compilers, and translators cited in the text. Numbers refer to page numbers.

A

Abshire, David M. 46
Adloff, Richard 43
Alexander, H.T. 45
Andemicael, Berhanykun 18
Arkhurst, Frederick S. 18
Attwood, William 59
Austin, Dennis 45
Ayih, Michel 79
Aynor, H. S. 24

B

Barber, James 24
Bell, J. Bowyer 11, 93
Bissell, Richard 23
Boutros-Ghali, Boutros 18
Bowman, Larry W. 18, 59
Brooks, Hugh C. 11
Brown, Douglas 24
Brown, Irene 24
Brownlee, Ian 106
Burrell, R.M. 12

C

Cabral, Amilcar 94
Carroll, Faye 25
Cervenka, Zdenek 18
Cesaire, Aime 12
Chaliand, Gerard 94

Chester, Edward W. 60
Chilcote, Ronald H. 39, 46
Cohn, Helen Desfosses 70, 79
Conover, Helen 99
Cooley, John K. 81
Cook, Mercer 44
Corbett, Edward M. 43
Cottrell, Alvin J. 12
Cowan, L. Gray 12
Crabb, Cecil V. 25
Crocker, Chester A. 13
Currie, David P. 19

D

Daggs, Elisa 106
Dale, Doris Cruger 99
Dale, Richard 21, 25, 99, 103
Davidson, Basil 95
Day, John 95
Dickie, John 108
Duffy, James 47
Duignan, Peter 99
Dumoga, John 13
Dumont, Rene 41

E

el-Ayouti, Yassin 11
Emerson, Rupert 15, 60

Author Index

F

Farajallah, Samaan Boutros 19
Ferkiss, Victor 13
Foltz, William J. 43
Forsyth, Frederick 25
Fung, Karen 109

G

Gardinier, David 103
Gerard-Libois, Jules 25
Gibson, Richard 85, 95, 116
Gifford, Prosser 103
Glickman, Harvey 104
Goldschmidt, Walter 60
Good, Robert C. 45
Green, Reginald H. 13
Gross, Ernest A. 95
Grundy, Kenneth W. 8, 85, 88, 89, 91, 92, 95-96, 116

H

Hall, Richard 26
Hamrell, Sven 79
Hance, William A. 57, 60
Handyside, Richard 94
Hargreaves, John D. 43
Hayford, Fred Kwesi 60
Hayter, Teresa 43
Hazlewood, Arthur 19
Henricksen, Thomas 47
Hevi, John Emmanuel 81
Hoskyns, Catherine 26
Hovet, Thomas, Jr. 19
Hughes, A.J. 20

I

Idang, Gordon J. 26
Ismael, Tarek Y. 26

J

Jansen, G.H. 1, 24, 27
Johns, David H. 11, 27
Johns, Sheridan 90, 96
Jones, Ruth 102
Jumba-Masagazi, A.H.D. 100

K

Kamarck, Andrew M. 14, 116
Kanet, Roger E. 79, 80
Kapungu, Leonard T. 20
Keatley, Patrick 20
Kennan, George F. 61
Kesteloot, Lilyan 14
Kirkwood, Kenneth 45
Kitchen, Helen 107
Klinghoffer, Arthur Jay 70, 80

L

Lake, Anthony 61
Larkin, Bruce D. 75, 76, 82, 91, 116
Lefever, Ernest W. 61
Legum, Colin 1, 20, 107, 116
Legvold, Robert 71, 80, 116
Leonhardt, Robert 94
Lewis, William H. 43
Louis, Wm. Roger 103
Lusignan, Guy de 44
Lystad, Robert A. 104

M

McGowan, Patrick J. 27
McKay, Vernon 14, 27
Marcum, John A. 61, 96
Marquard, Leo 20
Marshall, Charles Burton 61
Marvin, David K. 14
Mazrui, Ali A. 2, 14, 41
Melady, Thomas Patrick 62, 109
Meyers, B. David 21
Miller, J.D.B. 15
Minogue, Martin 100
Minter, William 47
Molloy, Judith 100
Mondlane, Eduardo 97
Moraes, Frank 15
Morgenthau, Ruth Schachter 44
Morison, David, 70, 80
Morris, Milton D. 70, 81
Morris, Roger 62
Morrison, Donald George 108
Morrow, John H. 62
Mortimer, Edward 44

Mushkat, Marion 21
Mutharika, B.W.T. 21
Mytelka, Lynn K. 101

N

Neres, Philip 44
Newbury, Colin W. 46
Nielsen, Waldemar A. 15, 38, 58, 62, 116
Nkrumah, Kwame 27
Nogueira, Alberto Franco 47

O

Okigbo, Pius N.C. 42
Ott, Phyllis Nauts 41

P

Padelford, Norman J. 15
Paden, John N. 101, 104
Park, Stephen 61
Pearson, J.D. 102
Pelissier, Rene 47
Pinkham, Joan 12
Pomeroy, William J. 63
Potholm, Christian P. 21, 99, 103

Q

Quaison-Sackey, Alex 16
Quigg, Philip W. 16

R

Rake, Alan 108
Rattray, David 94
Rivkin, Arnold 16, 42, 63
Rothchild, Donald S. 22

S

Said, Abdul A. 16
Samuels, Michael A. 46
Schatten, Fritz 70, 73, 81

Segal, Ronald 109
Seidman, Ann 13
Senghor, Leopold Sedar 44
Shepherd, George W., Jr. 28
Skurnik, W.A.E. 22, 28
Slawecki, Leon M.S. 82
Smaldone, Joseph P. 102
Smith, Stuart 63
Soja, Edward W. 101, 104
Stokke, Baard Richard 81
Stokke, Olav 97
Streeten, Paul 17

T

Tandon, Yashpal 86
Tareq, Ismael Y. 82
Tevoedjre, Albert 22
Thiam, Doudou 28
Thompson, Virginia 22
Thompson, W. Scott 7, 23, 28
Toure, Sekou 44-45

V

Vandenbosch, Amry 29
Venter, Al J. 97-98

W

Wallerstein, Immanuel 23
Weissman, Stephen R. 63
Welch, Claude E., Jr. 2, 23
Wheeler, Douglas L. 47
Widstrand, Carl Goesta 17, 79, 97
Williams, G. Mennen 63
Woronoff, Jon 7, 23

Y

Young, Rebecca 25

Z

Zartman, I. William 10, 17, 23, 42, 116

TITLE INDEX

This index includes all titles of books and published reports which are cited in the text. In most cases, the titles have been shortened. Journals, titles of articles, and chapter titles are not included. Numbers refer to page numbers.

A

Activities of Private U.S. Organizations in Africa 66
Addis Ababa Charter, The 18
Africa: Foreign Affairs Reader 16
Africa: Handbook 107
Africa: Politics 23
Africa and the Africans 63
Africa and the Challenge of Development 64
Africa and the Common Market 42
Africa and the European Common Market 42
Africa and the United States 60
Africa and the West 63
Africa and World Order 15
Africa Between East and West 13
Africa Contemporary Record 107
Africa in the Seventies and Eighties 18
Africa in the United Nations 19
Africa in World Politics 14
African Aims and Attitudes 100
African Battleline 62
African Boundary Problems 17
African Briefing--1968 64
African Diplomacy 27
African Experience, The. Vol. IIIA 101
African Experience, The. Vol. IIIB

104
African Integration and Disintegration 19
African Liberation Movements 85, 95
African Phenomenon, The 16
African Presence in World Affairs, The 16
African Profiles 109
African Programs of U.S. Organizations 110
African Refugee Problems 68
African Socialism 100
African Tightrope 45
Africa 71 105
Africa South of the Sahara 105
Africa's Search for Identity 13
Africa Unbound 16
Against the World 24
Aid to Africa 17
All Africa 106
American Foreign Policy 111
American Foreign Policy in the Congo 63
Angola 47
Angolan Revolution, The 96
Apartheid Axis 63
Armed Struggle in Africa 94

B

Background Notes 111

Basic Documents on African Affairs 106
Biafra Story, The 25
Bibliography of Africa, The 102
Black Africa 12
Black Africa: Handbook 108
Botswana and its Southern Neighbor 25
Briefing on Africa--1959 65, 66
Briefing on Africa--1960 65, 66
Britain and Africa 45
Britain and South Africa 45
Burundi 62
Business as Usual 61

C

Challenge of the Congo 27
China and Africa, 1949-1970 75, 76, 82, 91
Clash of Titans 60
Communism in Africa 70, 73, 81
Communist States and Developing Countries 78
Confrontation and Accommodation in Southern Africa 8, 88, 89, 95
Crisis in the African Drought, The 64
Crisis in the Congo 61
Crisis over Rhodesia 61
Critical Developments in Namibia 65
Current Bibliography on African Affairs, A 99
Current Foreign Policy 111

D

Dilemmas of African Independence, The 12
Directory of African Studies in the U.S. 106
Discourse on Colonialism 12
Dragon's Embrace, The 81
Dream of Unity 2, 24
Drought Crisis in the Sahel, The 64

E

East Africa 20
East Wind Over Africa 81

Economic Sanctions Against Rhodesia 66
Economics of African Development, The 14
Ein Afrikaner in Moskau 79
Elephants and the Grass, The 25
Emerging Africa in World Affairs 14
Ethiopia-Somalia-Kenya Dispute, The 26
Executive Agreements with Portugal and Bahrein 67
Expérience Guinéenne et Unité Africaine 44

F

Faces of Africa, The 64
False Start in Africa 41
Federalism and the New Nations of Africa 19
Federation of Southern Africa, A 20
First Ambassador to Guinea 62
Foreign Affairs Reader, A 16
Foreign Assistance Program, The 111
Foreign Policy Implications of Racial Exclusion in Granting Visas 64
Foreign Policy of African States, The 28
Foreign Policy of Senegal, The 28
France and the Africans 44
French Aid 43
French Presence in Black Africa, The 43
French-Speaking Africa 43
French-Speaking Africa Since Independence 44
French-Speaking West Africa from Colonial Status to Independence 44
From French West Africa to the Mali Federation 43
Future Direction of U.S. Policy Toward Southern Rhodesia 67

G

Geographic Bulletin 111
Ghana's Foreign Policy 28
GIST 111
Great Powers and Africa, The 15, 38, 58

Groupe Afro-Asiatique dans les
Nations Unies, Le   19
Growing Pains of Independence   12
Guerilla Struggle in Africa   85, 91,
92, 96
Guide to African Research and Refer-
ence Works   99

H

Handbook of African Affairs, A   107
Hearings. See specific title.
High Price of Principles, The   26
Horn of Africa, The   11

I

Immediate and Future Problems in the
Congo   64
Implementation of the U.S. Arms
Embargo   65
Implications for U.S. Legal Obliga-
. tions of the Presence of the
Rhodesian Information Office in
the U.S.   65
Importance of Being Black, The   15
Importation of Rhodesian Chrome   68
Indian Ocean--Political and Strategic
Future, The   67
Indian Ocean, The   12
Inside America   60
Intellectual Origins of the African
Revolution   14
International African Bibliography
100
International Nationalism   95
International Organization Series   111
International Politics of the Rhodesian
Rebellion, The   45
International Relations in the New
Africa   10, 23

K

Katanga Secession   25

L

Liberation of Guinea, The   95

M

Minority Rule and Refugees in Africa   64
Myth of the Guerilla, The   93

N

Nigeria   26
Nigerian-Biafran Relief Situation   68
Nomination of Nathaniel Davis to be
Assistant Secretary of State for
African Affairs   67
Nonaligned Black Africa   28
Nonalignment   1
Nonalignment and the Afro-Asian
States   27
Notes from Africa   24

O

On African Socialism   44
Organization of African Unity and its
Charter, The   18
Organizing African Unity   7, 23

P

Pan-Africanism   1, 20
Pan-Africanism in Action   22
Passing By   62
Peaceful Settlement Among African
States   18
Policy Toward Africa in the Seventies
65
Political Parties in French-Speaking
West Africa   44
Politics of Indifference, The   61
Politics of Partnership, The   20
Politics of the Third World, The   15
Politics of Trade Negotiations Between
Africa and the European Community,
The   42
Politique Internationale du Parti Démo-
cratique de Guinée, La   45
Portugal in Africa   47
Portugal's War in Guinea-Bissau   97
Portuguese Africa   39, 46
Portuguese Africa: Handbook   46
Portuguese Africa and the West   47

Title Index

Postwar Nigerian Situation, The 65
Profiles of African Leaders 109

R

Reds and the Blacks, The 59
Refugees South of the Sahara 11
Repeal of the Rhodesian Chrome
Amendment, The 67
Report and Hearings: Students 66
Report of a Special Study Mission to
Africa, Conducted by the Honorable
Barratt O'Hara, Illinois, Chairman
of the Subcommittee on Africa 66
Report of Special Factfinding Mission
to Nigeria 64
Report of Special Study Mission to
West and Central Africa 66
Report of the Special Coordinator for
Nigerian Relief 65
Report of the Special Study Mission
to Africa 64
Report of the Special Study Mission
to Africa, South and East of the
Sahara 67
Report of the Special Study Mission
to Southern Africa 64
Report on Portuguese Guinea and the
Liberation Movement 65
Report on United Nations Use of
Peacekeeping Forces in the Middle
East, The Congo, and Cyprus 64
Report on United States Foreign
Operations in Africa, A 67
Return to the Source 94
Review of State Department Trip
Through Southern and Central
Africa 65
Revolution in Guinea 94

S

Sahara, The 17
Sanctions as an Instrument of the
United Nations 66
South Africa and the World 29
South Africa and United States
Foreign Policy 65
South Africa's Foreign Policy 24
South Africa's Outward Strategy 59

Southern Africa: Vol. I 97
Southern Africa: Vol. II 97
Southern Africa and the United States
57, 60
Southern Africa in Perspective 21
South West Africa and the United
Nations 25
Soviet and East European Trade and
Aid in Africa 81
Soviet Bloc, China and Africa, The
79
Soviet Perspectives on African Socialism
80
Soviet Policy in West Africa 70, 80
Soviet Policy Toward Black Africa 70,
79
Spear and Scepter 61
State Department Bulletin 111
Struggle for Mozambique, The 97
Study Mission to Africa, Nov.-Dec.,
1960 68
Study Mission to Africa, Sept.-Oct.,
1961 67
Study Mission to Central and East
Africa, Feb. 1971 68
Sub-Saharan Africa 102

T

Terror Fighters, The 98
Third World, The 47
Toward Multinational Economic Co-
operation in Africa 21
Towards a Pax Africana 2, 14
Toward Unity in Africa 22

U

U.A.R. in Africa, The 26
United Nations and Africa 67
United Nations and Economic Sanctions
Against Rhodesia, The 20
United Nations Operations in the
Congo 66
United Nations Sanctions Against
Rhodesia: Chrome 67
United States and Africa, The 60
United States and Canadian Publica-
tions and Theses on Africa 103
United States Business Involvement in
Southern Africa 65

United States Foreign Policy: Africa 53, 67
United States Foreign Policy 1969-70 111
United States Foreign Policy 1971 112
United States Information Agency Operations in Africa 65
U.S. Neocolonialism in Africa 63
U.S. Security Agreements 56, 68
United States Security Agreements and Commitments Abroad 68
United States--South African Relations 66

Unity or Poverty 13
U.S.S.R. and Africa, The 70, 80

W

West Africa: Former 43
West Africa: French Speaking 43
West African Commonwealth, The 46
West Africa's Council of the Entente 22
Who's Who in Africa 108

SUBJECT INDEX

Underlined page numbers refer to areas of emphasis within the main subject heading. Alphabetization is letter by letter.

A

Addis Ababa Charter 18
Addis Ababa Conference 107
African Liberation Committee 86, 87
Afrikaans 107
African National Congress (South Africa) 88
African Bibliographic Center 88
Algeria 4, 50, 78, 87
Angola 57, 78, 86, 95, 97, 98, 102
Asia 36, 82, 104
Australia 54
Azores 58

B

Balewa, Sir Abubakar 26
Bandung conference of non-aligned nations 72, 74. See also Non-alignment
Bangla Desh 84
Belgium 26, 31, 40
Berlin 51
Biafra 25, 51, 84, 85
Brazil 47
Brazzaville Group 4
British West Africa 19
Burundi 40, 85

C

Cameroons 23, 102

Canada 99, 103, 107
Canary Islands 86, 95
Casablanca Group 4, 74
de Chardin, Pierre Teilhard. See Teilhard de Chardin, Pierre
China, People's Republic 10, 11, 15, 52, 69, 71, 74, 81, 82, 86, 87, 88, 90, 107
  policy in Africa 74-77, 79
  ideology 75-76
China, Republic of 75, 82
Chou En-lai 75
Christianity 12
Colonialism 2, 5, 12, 13, 14, 16, 100, 101. See also Neocolonialism
Communist states' policy 18
  military aid 13, 104
Comoro Islands 95, 102
Congo, ex-Belgian 4, 26, 27, 28, 40, 45, 50, 61, 74, 75, 106. See also Zaire
Cuba 51, 72

E

East Africa 7, 102, 105
Eastern Europe 59, 77, 81, 87
Economics 5-6, 7, 13-14, 16, 18
Egypt 27, 104
Eisenhower, Dwight D. 62
Entente, Council of the 22
Ethiopia 49, 53, 55, 56, 61, 77, 85, 102

Subject Index

Europe 99, 103, 104
   and colonialism 31, 32
   proper role in Africa 41
European Economic Community 40,
   41, 42, 63
Ewe 23

F

Fanon, Frantz 91
Foreign Affairs Research Coordinating
   Group 109
Foreign policy 8-11, 17, 22, 26,
   27, 28, 103. See also Inter-
   national relations
France 3, 4, 5, 13, 41, 43, 44,
   105, 109
   colonial policy 32-36, 37-39
   cultural relations 35, 38, 80
   defense policy 34, 35, 107
   economic policy 34, 40
Franco-Prussian War 31
French Territory of the Afar and
   Issa 31, 86, 95
French West Africa 3, 19, 22, 43

G

Gambia 23
Germany, West 13, 32, 40
Ghana 45, 53, 55, 61, 73, 74,
   102
Ghana-Guinea-Mali Union 23
Great Britain 3, 13, 31, 51, 95,
   105, 106
   colonial policy 35-39
   defense policy 36, 37
Guinea 44, 45, 55, 59, 62, 72,
   73, 74, 78
Guinea-Bissau 78, 83, 85, 86, 88,
   94, 95, 102

H

Houphouet-Boigny, Felix 23

I

Independence 3, 14, 16, 21, 28,
   32, 44, 73, 104, 106
India 9, 14, 36

Indian Ocean 74
Indochina 51
International Affairs Institute 100
International Association for the Development of Libraries in Africa
   105
International Relations 101, 103, 104,
   105, 106, 107
   conflict patterns 9-10
   diplomacy 11, 27
   ideology 10, 15, 23
   inter-African disputes 6, 26
   security 16, 107
   systems theory 8, 18, 103
   unification 15, 18, 19, 20, 22,
     23, 27, 101
   See also Foreign policy
Israel 9, 21, 24, 104, 107
Ivory Coast 9, 22, 44

J

Japan 105

K

Katanga 25
Kaunda, H. Kamuzu 26
Kennedy, J.F. 53, 59
Kenya 20, 53, 59
Krushchev, Nikita 50, 53, 71, 72,
   73, 80

L

Lesotho 102
Liberation movements 28, 96, 108
   classification 85-86
   external support 86-88
   information by 102
   nature of conflicts 84-85
   theories of warfare 90-92, 94, 96
   views of conflicts 83-84
Liberia 49, 53, 55
Library of Congress 102
Lumumba, Patrice 40
Lusaka Manifesto 106

M

Madagascar 104, 105

Malawi 20
Mali Federation 3, 43, 44
Mali Republic 55, 73, 74
Marshall Plan 52
Mauritania 4
Mauritius 105
Middle East 7, 10, 74, 77, 82
Morocco 4, 17
Mozambique 57, 78, 86, 95, 97,
    102

N

Namibia 57, 102. See also South
    West Africa
Nasser, Gamal Abdel 27
Nationalism 13
Nazi Germany 70
Neocolonialism 5-6, 110. See also
    Colonialism
Neutralism 6, 16. See also Non-
    alignment
Neutrality 6
Newson, David 53
Nigeria 19, 26, 49, 53, 54, 55,
    78, 105
Nkrumah, Kwame 16, 28, 74, 100
Nonalignment 6, 8, 11, 24, 25, 27,
    28, 51, 104. See also Neutral-
    ism

O

Oceania 54
Office of External Research 109
Organisation Commune africaine,
    malgache, et mauricienne 4-5,
    108
Organization of African Unity 4-5,
    6-7, 8, 9, 15, 18, 19, 21,
    22, 23, 62, 74, 88, 92, 99,
    107, 108, 111

P

Pan-Africanism 1-29, 100, 103, 104
    definition 1, 2, 16
    See also International Relations:
    conflict patterns, unification;
    Organization of African Unity

Peace Corps 52, 53
Philippines 51
Portugal 7, 32, 54, 56, 83, 85, 87,
    96, 97
    colonial policy 38-40, 46, 47
Portuguese Territories 5, 31, 62, 85,
    86, 87, 92, 93, 95, 102, 108

R

Refugees 11-12
Rhodesia 5, 19, 20, 24, 28, 36, 37,
    51, 52, 54, 57, 58, 61, 62,
    83, 85, 86, 88, 93, 95, 102,
    105, 109. See also Zimbabwe
Rosenau, James N. 27, 28
Rumania 107
Russia 6, 10, 12, 13, 14 '.., 51,
    52, 59, 69, 86, 89. See also
    Soviet Union

S

Sahara Desert 17
Sao Tome e Principe 95
Scandinavia 88, 97
School of Oriental and African Studies
    100
Second World War 31, 32, 33, 36,
    60, 80
Senegal 3-4, 28, 35, 44, 55, 87
Senghor, Leopold Sedar 22
Serials 105
Socialism 16, 28
Socialist States
    economic policy 77-80
    security policy 78
Somalia 77
Soudan 3-4, 44, 55
South Africa, Republic of 7, 17, 18,
    37, 45, 52, 54, 58, 60, 62,
    63, 71, 83, 85, 86, 88, 89,
    93, 95, 102, 105, 106, 108
    foreign policy 24, 96
South Asia 77
South Atlantic Ocean 54
Southeast Asia 51
Southern Africa 49, 53, 57, 58, 59
South West Africa 25, 52, 58, 62,
    86, 93, 95, 105. See also
    Namibia

Sovereignty 9, 12
Soviet Union 79, 81, 87, 88, 105,
   107
   analytical problems 69-71
   and African socialism 73, 80
   ideology 72-73
   policy in Africa 71-74
   See also Russia
Spain 30
Spanish Sahara 31
de Spinola, General Antonio 97
Stalin, Joseph 71, 80
Stanleyville paratroop drop 100
Sudan 27, 55, 78, 85, 86
Suez Canal 37
Swaziland 93, 102
Sweden 87
Switzerland 40
Syria 102

T

Tanganyika 20. See also Tanza-
   nia
Tanzania 53, 78
Tanzania/Zambia railroad 77, 78
Teilhard de Chardin, Pierre 13
Territory of the Afar and Issa. See
   French Territory of the Afar
   and Issa
Togo 78
Toure, Sekou 72
Tshombe, Moise 4

U

Uganda 20, 53, 108
Union africaine et malgache 24
United Nations 4, 5, 14, 15, 16,
   18, 25, 26, 37, 39, 45, 50,

   51, 52, 53, 58, 59, 61, 62,
   74, 84, 88, 95, 105, 106, 111
Afro-Asian Group 19, 27
Economic Commission for Africa 17
Economic and Social Council 20
General Assembly 19
United States 14, 15, 16, 25, 28,
   41, 47, 89, 95, 99, 110
   bibliographic services 102, 103,
   105
   Congress 57, 58
   economic relations 52-54, 111
   New realism 52
   policy determinants 49-50
   policy periods 51-52
   security policy 54-56
   and southern Africa 56-58, 89
Upper Volta 55

V

Vietnam 36, 59
Vorster, John B. 88

W

West Africa 22, 24
Western Europe 12, 28, 50, 51, 107
World Council of Churches 87
World War II. See Second World War

Z

Zaire 40, 49, 55, 61. See also
   Congo, ex-Belgian
Zambia 20, 26, 45, 57, 77, 87
Zanzibar 20, 102
Zimbabwe 102. See also Rhodesia
Zimbabwe African National Union 88
Zulu 107